Saved *from* Silence

Saved *from* Silence

Finding Women's Voice in Preaching

Mary Lin Hudson
Mary Donovan Turner

Chalice Press
St. Louis, Missouri

Biblical quotations, unless otherwise noted, are from the *New Revised Standard Version Bible*, copyright 1989, Division of Christian Education of the National Council of Churches of Christ in the USA. Used by permission.

Cover: Judy Newell
Interior design: Elizabeth Wright

This book is printed on acid-free, recycled paper.

Visit Chalice Press on the World Wide Web at
www.chalicepress.com

10 9 8 7 6 5 4 3 2 1   99 00 01 02 03

Library of Congress Cataloging–in–Publication Data

Turner, Mary Donovan.
    Saved from silence : finding women's voice in preaching / by Mary Donovan Turner and Mary Lin Hudson.
        p.   cm.
    ISBN 0-8272-3439-2
    1. Preaching.   2. Feminism—Religious aspects—Christianity. Women clergy.
I. Hudson, Mary Lin.
    BV4235.F44T87   1999   9921267
                                                        CIP ′

Printed in the United States of America

Dedicated to Our parents
Mary Alice England Hudson and John L. Hudson
Mary Folk Donovan and Lewis Grant Donovan

Table of Contents

Acknowledgments

Coming to voice has been, and will continue to be, a lifelong experience. Many people along the way, both family and friends, have been an important part of that journey with us. We are grateful for their support and challenge.

Our institutions, the Pacific School of Religion and Memphis Theological Seminary, granted us sabbatical leaves for finishing the manuscript. Our colleagues at each of these institutions have given encouragement and counsel through the various stages of conversation about "voice." Archie Smith, Jr., and Mitzi Minor have offered endless support through conversation and reading various versions of the manuscript. Thanks go to the members of the "writing group" at PSR—Joe Driskill, Jeffrey Kuan, and Sharon Thornton—who know full well the joy and agony of putting word on page, and to Area VII colleagues at the Graduate Theological Union, particularly those in homiletics—Jana Childers, Linda Clader, and Tom Rogers—who have offered continuing reassurance. Diane Oliver, Donald McKim, and Evelyn McDonald have also supported our work. A special thanks to David and Betty Buttrick for time away at the cabin. For all of these, we are grateful.

The research for this study would not have been as complete without the aid of Alexis Solomon, research assistants at PSR, and the resourceful library staff at Memphis Theological Seminary. In addition, Audrey Englert and the clerical staff at PSR have offered assistance in the physical challenge of pumping words into computer and onto printed page. The valuable offerings of Cheryl Cornish, Cynthia Okayama Dopke, Olivia Latu, Sharon Lewis Karamoko, Margaret McKee, Rosalyn Nichols, Alexis Solomon, Almella Starks-Umoja, and Cheryl Ward have added fresh voices to our work. Jon L. Berquist has been a helpful and supportive editor.

We are particularly grateful for permission from Beverly Wildung Harrison to share her story in this volume. Her comments gave clarity and strength to that section.

To our families, who tolerated our nearly singular focus on this manuscript as it came to conclusion, we recognize the sacrifices you have made so that we could complete this work. Lamar, Erin, Chris, Suzanne, Mary Alice and Sue Beth have patiently encouraged and consoled at the most crucial times.

Someone once advised us that if we wanted to remain friends, we should never write a book together. It is true that writing is stressful. The journey together, however, has been mostly surprising, enriching, and full of grace. We are grateful, even now, to claim each other as friend.

Prelude

Leaning over cups of coffee in a busy metropolitan airport, we contemplated a puzzling event that had taken place during a recent preaching class. A student stood before her peers dressed in appropriate vestments. Her manuscript, prepared with care, was centered neatly on the pulpit. The sermon was finely crafted, full of vivid images and forceful theological implications for the church. She had something important to say. Yet, when she opened her mouth, little more than a faint whisper was heard. The preacher had no voice. As preaching professors, we analyzed the student's experience and the classes in homiletics that we both had taught. We realized that most students prepare for preaching by focusing on the development of skills for interpreting texts and crafting sermons to the neglect of a much deeper concern: the relationship of the student's own voice to the proclamation of the gospel. This conversation gave birth to our interest in the meaning of "voice."

As we continued to contemplate the relationship between voice and preaching, our second, wider conversation began to occur with other faculty members, ministers, and friends. Walking through the faculty secretary's office on a Monday afternoon, Mary Donovan Turner sat down at a table with a colleague, who asked about her current writing project. She simply said, "I'm working on voice." His eyes lit up with enthusiasm, and the conversation exploded with quick and forceful exchanges about voice and ethics, voice and suffering, voice and name. In a matter of minutes, a vast array of meanings and significance attached to voice were discovered. The Hispanic colleague revealed that he was trying to recapture his once-fluent facility with the Spanish language. Early in his childhood he had learned not to speak Spanish in a public place; it was not as valued as English. By learning Spanish once again, he was recapturing an important part of his voice. This conversation and many others throughout the following months substantiated what we had instinctively known: the concept of voice deserved greater attention.

As our awareness of the concept increased, we began to find "voice" everywhere. The metaphor of voice was discovered to be alive and well in every academic discipline. It had become a metaphor of choice for many theologians, ethicists, literary critics, biblical scholars, pastoral care providers, and the like. All were talking about "finding voice" and "claiming voice." Moreover, when a person previously denied or discounted in a field of study made contributions, they were dubbed "voices from the margin." Recognition of the "voices of the silenced" began to emerge. We also discovered, in a new way, that the metaphor had become a part of the homiletic community's shared vocabulary.

Since the 1970s the metaphor of voice has inundated both public and private discourse. The emergence of its use coincided with the cultural changes that followed the civil rights and women's liberation movements in North American history. "Voice" as a metaphor corresponds to basic principles in feminist, womanist, and liberationist thought that recognize the issues of power and oppression in relationships. Its polyvalent dimensions have allowed all of those who had been considered "other" to adopt it as a means of symbolizing and depicting their value in our pluralistic, postmodern world.

This recognition and awareness of the widespread use of "voice" launched us, Mary and Mary Lin, on a great adventure. We have discovered the important understandings of "voice" within the great stories of redemption and liberation recorded in the Old and New Testaments. We have scoured writings of the leaders of the Reformation, as well as the works of current homileticians for their understandings of "voice" in relation to preaching. We have unearthed examples of women who found "voice" in the face of great opposition and resistance. In addition, we have looked carefully at the contemporary woman's experience. Our research has reinforced our belief that recognizing and understanding "voice" is not just important, but mandatory, as those previously denied access to the pulpit come to take their places there.

What we write is, in a sense, autobiographical. As women, we know about silence and voice in their manifold dimensions. We know what it is like to "lose voice" in the movement from childhood to adolescence. We know what it is like to "desperately seek our voices" as women called to ministry; to "talk back" as "radical feminists" in conservative environments has been an experience of resistance and pain for each of us. To embody "voice" as friend, preacher, professor, and singer has brought joy.

Mary knows what it is like to come face-to-face with the possibility of the silence of death, only to be brought back to life, and ultimately to speech.

The words we write reflect the struggles of others, women and men alike. When we have shared our thoughts with ministers who, because of gender or orientation are still denied the opportunity to bring a word to the gathered community, they simply respond by quietly saying, "Yes. That is my story."

We believe it is a story that needs to be told.

Mary Lin Hudson
Mary Donovan Turner
November 20, 1998

Introduction

Saved from Silence. Before this volume had thesis, scope, method, or form, it had this title. The phrase has stubbornly persisted throughout seasons of conversation, growth, reevaluation, and change. *Saved from Silence.* From the beginning this title spoke to us clearly and powerfully; only in the months and then years that followed were we to discover why. Although this book focuses on preaching, it has been first and foremost about us, we who are continually in the process of being saved.

The volume you now hold in your hands did not come easily; it has been a costly endeavor. It is a product of our own remembering and sharing. There has often been compromise in our thinking. Yet, without failure, each conversation has brought new questions that have led us to horizons we first had not visualized and sounds that were before unheard. Our conversations with others, whose experiences were both like and unlike our own, opened new dimensions in understanding that led us down new corridors of questions, chaos, and promise.

This volume has an itinerary. It takes you where the journey first led us. We will point out the interesting places along the way, although we can't linger at any of them. We hope the "stops" along the tour will encourage you to visit again.

The journey begins with the task of defining the metaphorical term "voice." Metaphorical language opens into a variety of meanings, based upon the context in which it is used. The use of metaphor is central to the task of preaching, just as the parables were central to the ministry of Jesus. In this volume, we use "voice" as our root metaphor. It is a way to think about the theological foundations that give preaching coherence and meaning. Metaphor is an integral part of the human experience of emotions, thought, speech, and action. It is a way of knowing that expands our understanding of reality and enables us to see something new by referring to something familiar. This is especially significant when referring to religious metaphors, or naming the ways God is present in our experiences.[1]

For our purposes, we wanted the definition of "voice" to be broad enough to be inclusive of the experience of all human beings. At the same time, we wished to narrow the definition to those meanings that would address the concerns of women and preaching. How would we define the term "voice" for this study?

No metaphor is complete. No metaphor reflects the totality of that which it represents. Inevitably, a metaphor highlights important characteristics and diminishes others. We are aware of this metaphor's limitations and dangers. There are some in our world who do not know, for a variety of reasons, the physical capacity for speech. Thus, to use "voice" as metaphor to describe our ability to express ourselves and make a difference in the world may seem to these, at least, foreign, if not exclusive of their own life experiences. Our hope is that these women and men can relate to struggles that are different from and, at the same time, like their own: the struggle to claim the value that is inherently ours because we are created by and in the image of God; the struggle to bring one's self to the fullest expression possible; the struggle to wrest ourselves from the gut-wrenching agony of being "other." We extend the possibility that the metaphor of voice can represent all of our ways of making ourselves known in the world—through physical voice, but also through movement, gesture, and other forms of expression.

Our curiosity about voice and its metaphorical power took us to biblical texts, the source that has often been used to silence the persons who are our intended readers. Yet intuitively, we knew that the gospel had something to do with voice and silence. The connection, we thought, was strong; it was ultimate. What happens, we asked, when we take our own experience and those of other women born in a particular place and time and put them in conversation with the texts of our tradition? We were not seeking validation for our own experience. Rather, we were searching for the threads about voice within the tradition, wondering how they looked when pulled together into one place. There, in the language and struggle of faith, we found "voice" and "silence" in others' expressions and words. But we found more. We found in the biblical texts a model for ongoing interpretation that demands that the contextualized voice speak to its world. We found a hermeneutic that makes our own engagement with the text—because it is ours—important and necessary.

We brought our questions. What does the text say about the voiced and listening God? What does it say about the voiced and listening people? What does voice have to do with covenant and community? When does the human word become God's word, or when does God's word become human? This search was revelatory. It called for response. It was liberating. Listening to the voice of God roaring from Mount Horeb and watching

God's spirit continually and consistently bring ordinary people of the early church to speech awakened and renewed in us the desire to be voiced women, voiced preachers. It made us aware that to silence voices is doing more than oppressing; it is stifling a creature's god-likeness. Gradually as we read narrative, lament, law, and prophetic speech, our own theology came into being. We synthesized both thought and feeling to form and fashion an unsystematic, flexible, dynamic theological statement that gives foundation to a "voiced" homiletic.

It is not enough to speak only in the abstract. Good preachers know that is true. So our journey took us on an historical adventure; we needed bodies, the real bodies of women. We explored the lives of particular women in the early church, the Middle Ages, the nineteenth and twentieth centuries. These "leaps" through time did not accord us a complete or holistic picture of the struggle of women throughout the ages. Rather, they illustrated graphically how the struggles of individual women to become voiced have a particularity born out of human life context. Alas, we wished we could gather these women together to see what they could learn from each other. Perhaps they would learn as much from each other as we had learned from them.

It would be easy to be deceived into believing that the struggles of the women of the past were not now our own. We could believe that the demons have been slain, the obstacles overcome, the future opened wide for women in the church. Sadly, it is not so. Our journey took us to the worlds of psychology and social analysis, where we discovered the increasing amount of work being done on women's experience. We delved into the many studies of adolescent girls and women that demonstrate the varied and dramatic ways they are silenced. We acknowledged the ways the church coconspires with society in this. In doing so, we found a pervasive and persistent cloud that dampens, covers, and silences. What happens when the woman who has learned not to value her own thoughts, emotions, and experiences is called to preach? Where does the teaching of preaching begin? How does she learn to value what she has to say? How can women move into the world of preaching to bring the prophetic word? How are they themselves the prophetic word? How can they be "saved from silence?" The implications of this theology of voice for preaching and the teaching of it are immense and brimming with promise.

This journey through the worlds of the Old Testament and the New, through the venues of theology, history, sociology, and psychology led ultimately to the contemporary world of the preacher. Knowing that truth emerges in conversation among diverse "voices" and that human experiences are indeed revelatory, we gathered from our respective communities (Memphis Theological Seminary and Pacific School of Religion) two groups of women to reflect upon a list of theological affirmations about voice. How did these women understand God as voice? Was this metaphor helpful and consistent with their own understandings and experiences of God? How did they understand their own voices in the world? When had they known "voice" and "silence"? How did these experiences inform their own theologies of preaching, and how did their preaching experiences inform their relationship and reactions to the metaphor?

The two conversations took place on the same day, August 13, 1998, although on different sides of the country. Gathering with Mary Lin was a group of five women—three African American and two European American. Three were pastors, one an associate pastor, and one a retired hospital chaplain. With Mary, there were four women—one African American, one European American, one Asian American and one Pacific Islander from Tonga. One was a pastor of a local congregation, one an associate pastor, one seeking employment as a teacher, and one a student at PSR. The group members came from various denominational backgrounds. Some were new to ministry, whereas others were looking back over many years of service. (See appendix A for more information about these women.)

In both groups, the stories that were told varied one from another, yet there were some common threads that bound them together. Some came wondering why they had been chosen for the discussion. Others came affirming the theological claims we had made about voice (See appendix B.) Still others had questions. All came to the table willingly and enthusiastically, remembering the stories of women past and present. Some found themselves speaking aloud for the first time their own life stories. Excerpts from these conversations are presented in "sidebars" throughout the volume. The sidebars contain the initials of the women speaking, so that they can be identified. These women's insights have both affirmed and challenged some of the assumptions that were foundational to our work. On both counts we have benefited from the conversation.

How can we understand the world that silences and how do we then understand theologically what it means to speak? Our conversations around the table have sparked new answers to very old questions. We know that this conversation is only a beginning. Further dialogue with women and men inside and outside seminary walls and churches will bring more fullness, wholeness to this conversation. And so, it is our hope that as a result of this study, others will be led to sit down around the table and hear each other into speech. Perhaps they, too, will experience something of what it means to be "saved from silence."

The voice is a poor miserable thing, to be reckoned as the least of creatures, not more than a breath of wind. As soon as the mouth ceases speaking, the voice is gone and is no more, so that there can be nothing weaker or more perishable. Yet it is so mighty, that I could rule a whole country with my voice.

Martin Luther[1]

Is it not indicative that the word for mask, persona (that through which the sound comes) has given both to the ancients and to us the word for person?

Walter Ong[2]

A presence is never mute.

Pierre Teilhard de Chardin, S.J.[3]

I want to posit the possibility that there is a word, that there are so many words, awaiting woman speech. And perhaps there is a word that has not yet come to sound—a word that once we begin to speak will round out and create deeper experience for us and put us in touch with sources of power, energy of which we are just beginning to become aware.

Nelle Morton[4]

Chapter 1

Voice as Emerging Metaphor

As an elementary school child in Shreveport, Louisiana, Mary heard the word "environment" for the first time. She was proud of having learned a long and important word, a word she assumed must have been known by only a privileged few. She was pleased to be one of them. Her awareness of the new word "environment," however, eventually proved her assumption wrong. Now recognizing the word, Mary found it everywhere she turned: on television, in sermons, in books, in ordinary day-to-day conversation. Although knowing this new word opened to her a world of meaning, she was slightly disappointed to find that almost everyone seemed to know it. Soon "environment" became to her an old, familiar friend. It found its place in her world of speech and discourse.

The experience of learning a new word, only to find it has already saturated the world around us, has repeated itself hundreds of times. The experience took on new drama when, together, Mary Lin and Mary focused their attention on the word "voice." Certainly they had heard the word since childhood. Their new attention to "voice" as a metaphor, however, led them to find it in their fields of study and elsewhere. What is it about "voice" that makes it such a multifaceted metaphor of human experience? Perhaps it is the complexity of the human voice that extends possibilities of meaning in so many different directions.

Human Voice as Metaphor

Speak aloud a simple phrase: "Hello! How are you?" This seemingly simple act requires little or no reflection. And yet, using the voice in this particular way involves the instantaneous integration of many different tasks. Voice, as embodied expression, becomes a place where the physical and the spiritual meet.

The act of speaking begins with breath. Human beings breathe in and out all the time, an involuntary reflex that engages the nose, mouth, muscles, lungs, heart, and blood. The most basic act of life itself is the flow of air into the body and its expulsion back into the atmosphere. In the Hebrew language, the words "breath," "wind," and "spirit" are all translations of the same word, *ruach*. As breath passes in and out of the body, a rhythm and flow is created that, like spirit, gives life.[5]

In order for sound to be produced, however, that "spirit" must meet and move the body's vocal cords. With the creation of a small vacuum, the cords are pulled together again after having been pushed apart, producing a vibrating pattern. These vibrations carry the energy of one's being into the universe through sound.

Sound emitted by the vocal cords is amplified when it passes through the rest of the body. The physical experience of speaking includes an awareness of sound resonating through various parts. Through the movement of lips, tongue, soft palate, and facial muscles this sound is transformed to speech.

None of these activities would be possible without some form of stimulation from the brain. The area of the brain that controls motor function must work in tandem with the area that is concerned with articulation, inflection, and vocabulary. It is in the cooperation of brain, breath, and body that voice results. These three discrete aspects of one's being must be integrated in order to produce the human voice. Within the interrelationship of brain, breath, and body, a distinctive quality of sound is produced that can be recognized in its uniqueness.[6]

Relating the voice to the concept of self, then, is not surprising. Few activities require such a totality of being as does speaking. Within every voice is the effort of a human being to express self. Voice signals the presence of the one who speaks. Not only does the sound of a voice affect the one who hears it; the speaker is affected also. As people vocalize their experiences, they learn about themselves, others, and the world. This action, produced by the integrated effort of body, breath, and brain, has the capacity to bring forth the deepest and most intimate expressions of the soul.

> I believe that when you speak, there is an energy or authority that you release. It's like a snowball. Metaphysically we create reality.
>
> ASU

A human being may be a single entity, but with many dimensions.[7] Using the metaphor of voice, these dimensions of the self may be expressed in ways that disclose the wide range of meaning that has come to be associated with the term. Some of the more prominent uses of the metaphor reveal dimensions of self that are distinctive, authentic, authoritative, resistant, and relational, inviting community and dialogue.

This constellation of meanings contributes a new framework for understanding the experiences of those who have been marginalized from the pulpit. As such, each of these five dimensions finds a place of importance in this exploration of a theology of preaching.

Voice as Distinctive Self

As individuals, we speak in voices that are uniquely our own. Around 4:30 one Saturday morning, I received a phone call from a man. I did not recognize his voice, so I assumed that I did not know him. He said, "Are you Mary Turner?" I told him that I was. After a long pause, he said, "Are you Mary E. Turner?" I answered, "No." He said, "I knew it." Again a long silence. I said to him, "Are you all right?" He said, "No. I haven't seen my mother in thirty years. I want to talk to her. I've called all the Mary Turners in the phone book. You're the last one. I knew by your voice that you were not the Mary Turner I needed to hear." The man who had not heard the voice of his mother in thirty years knew that if he heard it, he would recognize it.

Our distinctive voices are remarkably consistent over time and place. We identify people and recognize them by their voices. Maya Angelou's voice will never be mistaken for Barbra Streisand's. That is clear. Fred Craddock would never be confused with David Buttrick, and vice versa. Moreover, we know that it is not our perception of those voices alone that differs.[8] Fred Craddock and Maya Angelou have demonstrably unique voices—a voice print as clear and definitive as a finger print. The voice print may be captured by a computer synthesizer or a magnetic tape recording, but the pattern, tone, and nuances of that voice are uniquely reflective of the person who uttered the sound.

While voice prints are a recent discovery, the fact that voices are distinctive is not. That recognition provides the foundation for the story in the Hebrew scriptures of the aging, blind Isaac. As Isaac lies in his bed close to death, a person approaches claiming to be his firstborn son, Esau. Isaac is blind but still able to hear. Isaac senses that the voice is that of Jacob; he has long been able to distinguish one son's voice from the other, probably since birth.

Voice, then, not only symbolizes the self; it symbolizes a distinctive, unique self. Although the voice can change its pitch, pace, and inflection, reflecting a seemingly endless variety of emotions and feelings, there is a recognizable quality to it. The voice is wedded to each person in a way that is particular and undeniable.

Acknowledging the distinctiveness of the voice in the midst of a diverse community, the authors of *Hispanic Women: Prophetic Voice in the Church* intentionally chose to employ the metaphor of "voice" as a symbol of the diversity and distinctiveness in the Hispanic community. They interviewed as many diverse "voices" as possible—Mexican Americans, Puerto Ricans, and Cubans. They heard from voices of different classes, different educational backgrounds, younger and older women, women involved in church, and those for whom the church is only a peripheral reality.[9] The authors knew that each "voice" could and would present reality in a distinctive way. Each voice was an important part of the whole chorale of understanding.

The metaphor of voice affirms and values our diverse and distinctive selves, allowing for particularity and contextuality. This is in contrast to a singularly voiced reality that assumes that all persons experience life in the same way. This monotone perspective assumes a position of privilege over other views. When distinctiveness is recognized and valued, the horizons of reality are broadened and truth becomes multidimensional. Stifling distinctive voices incorrectly alters the world's vision.

The recognition of the distinctiveness of voice, then, has much to say about the importance of reconsidering the question of which persons are allowed to preach. How is the church's consciousness altered when diverse voices are stifled? How does the recognition of our distinctiveness help us understand the important role of the preacher in speaking to a particular community? How does the preacher's life experience inform and shape the word in particular and compelling ways? Is the distinctive voice a reflection of our godlikeness?

Voice as Authentic Self

Authentic voice refers to the level of consistency and appropriateness in the expression of a particular aspect of self in any given situation. Voice, as an expression of authentic self, can be recognized both in its distinctiveness from other voices and in its consistency within a given context. "Truth is a function of the stable individual's seeking to square the writing with the self," states one literary critic. "When the self is so found and so revealed in text, authenticity results."[10]

During a meeting of a basic preaching class, the students were asked to share a time in their lives when they felt "voiced" or "silenced." The students seemed to need no other instruction, but immediately began to relate stories about home, school, and church life. Some of them told of triumphant victories, and some told of painful times when they were not allowed to speak, or when they were not heard. One particular student recalled a conversation in which a close friend had shared the intimate details of a tragic event in his life. "I sat there with him," the student reflected. "I was totally present with him. I was silent…but in my silence, I have never been more voiced." Silence expressed a profound quality of being in that particular moment. The student recognized that his expression of silence was consistent with the truth that was embodied in that moment of relationship. That consistency represents authentic voice.

To express oneself authentically is neither simple nor clear. How do we evaluate our own authenticity? Authentic with which of our currently conflicting selves? Once we have found our authentic voice, will we ever lose it?

The authentic self does not have to express all or tell all at once, nor can it.[11] The authentic voice does, however, offer the possibility of extending the presence of truth between persons in relationship, allowing the truth to surface where it will and to do its work in the lives of those who allow it. A wise woman once claimed that real intimacy requires truth, and truth can only arise from an authentic self.[12]

Voice reflects a valuing of the self in relation to particular contexts, allowing authentic dimensions of the self to arise to expression rather than be submerged in a sea of competing expectations and roles. The valuing of context over self, in contrast, fosters particular roles for persons so that the self is masked and unrecognizable. Voice as metaphor affirms the freedom of expression by human beings in relationship.

The goal of being a fully functioning human being in the world requires the work of integration through continuing growth and development. This integration is a process of coming to one's authentic self in relation to other selves, community, and God. Therefore, the concept of "voice" as authentic expression is all about moving toward human wholeness.

It amazes me how deeply the process runs. I have been preaching every week for the past 3 years. Now, I'm still revisiting the issue of voice. In twenty years I hope and trust and pray that I will know more about my own experience so that I can articulate it clearly, freely, and confidently.

CC

How does one foster this integration with God that leads to authenticity? How is an authentic voice also faithful? How is the expression of authenticity experienced as liberation or redemption?

Voice as Authoritative Expression

Exercising the right to speak says something about the power and value of authorizing one's own perspective. To be author of our own reality is to claim the value of our experience, to trust our ability to reason and reflect, and to accept ourselves as we really are. This is central to the meaning of "voice" as authoritative expression.

In the volume *In Our Own Voices*, Ruether and Keller state that voice has become the metaphor of choice for women's efforts to speak and act as persons with authority in their own right. As the authors chronicle the contributions to religion that women in America have made, they use this metaphor. They tell of Anne Hutchinson, in 1637, who spoke with her own voice, claiming to have received a revelation from God. She was excommunicated from the Massachusetts Bay Colony because the clergy felt themselves to be the only authoritative mediators of God's word. The authors also speak of Sally Priesand who gained her voice when she became the first rabbi ordained in the Reform movement of Judaism in 1972. Other stories told by Ruether and Keller are as diverse as these, but they all reflect the efforts of women throughout history in taking an authoritative stance that defined life from their own perspectives—perspectives worthy of expression. Each woman "found her voice" in her own way. Through speech and action, each spoke an authoritative word.[13]

The use of the metaphor "voice" to represent the authoritative or valued self suggests that the voiced woman is one who recognizes her own value and thus accords herself the right to speak. Other people may feel authorized by a community that values their voices and listens to them.

This contemporary story illustrates the importance of authority in "voice." Through his ministry at a downtown church in Memphis, Tennessee, Doug had been involved in a street ministry for a number of years. He became acquainted with Charlie, a homeless man suffering from years of alcohol abuse. One day Doug received a call that Charlie was hemorrhaging to death. Because Doug was well respected in the community and because some of his parishioners worked in the ER of the regional medical center, Doug was able to call ahead and alert the staff that he was bringing in a man who needed immediate care. When he arrived at the hospital, the waiting room was packed with people waiting to be served. Doug's friend was treated immediately, however. With no empty examining rooms, the staff stretched Charlie out on the floor and began administering the needed drugs. As this was happening, an older African American woman approached Doug and tugged at his sleeve. She was accompanied by another woman and a pregnant teenager. "Father, it is good that you are here to get this man some help." Doug didn't know what kind of response she was expecting, so he replied, "I try to do what I can." She said, "I hope you never become poor." "Why?" he asked, a bit puzzled. "Because," she explained, "when you become poor you lose your voice."[14]

In the documentary *The Songs are Free,* Bernice Johnson Reagon reflects on the power that is carried in the human voice. "Singing," she claims, "announces our existence. To sing or speak is to say to the world, 'I am.' You can't ignore me or overlook me. I am here."[15] To some extent, the human voice is an instrument of power, a means of influencing others and the world. "Voice" implies a power inherent in self-expression that is born out of a sense of the value of authentic human experience in community.

Voice has value. How does one marginalized from the pulpit find the strength to value her voice amidst an environment hostile to it? How is God the author of the *authoritative* voice?

Voice as Resistant Self

"Finding a Voice: Coming to Terms with Contradictions" is the subheading of an essay on the power of self-definition. The author, Patricia Hill Collins, articulates the core theme in Black feminist thought as "finding a voice to express a self-defined Black woman's standpoint."[16] She suggests that the transformation from victim to survivor has to do with being able to use the range of one's voice. The metaphor of "voice" is related to the process by which one can come to define one's self, rather than being at the mercy of the system, which may create negative definitions or simply name a person as "other." When women have found voice, they have been able to make this important move from objectification to internally defined self-images. As a result, these women can "talk back." This voice has wrested the Black woman from invisibility.

Our culture says that women don't have anything to say. Only the male voice has power and substance. As women, we grow up in that culture. It claims us.

SLK

The metaphor expresses the triumph of the oppressed coming to personhood, freedom, and power in a world that has sought to silence them. Voice calls attention to the pain and suffering of the individual and community; criticizes oppression; offers and demands solutions; cries out in passion, anger, and outrage; shocks and touches; changes attitudes, social customs, and practice; motivates reform; calls people out to radical and revolutionary action; and resists systems of injustice.[17]

It is difficult to imagine feminism devoid of the metaphor of "voice." Within the world of feminist, womanist, and mujerista thought, almost every use of the metaphor is related to a woman's coming to terms with her self in light of the oppressive structures around her. For instance, Carol Gilligan's *In a Different Voice* praises the nurturing and relational discourse culturally marked by and for women. bell hooks in *Talking Back* speaks about "voice" that is engaged, that interrogates differences. In *Silences,* Tillie Olsen laments conditions that prevent women from giving voice to their own life experiences.[18] Each of these works draws on the metaphor of "voice," because these women have experienced restrictions to their voicing of opinion, experience, analysis, and passions because of their positions in the social order. The voice, provoked by pain or joy, can eclipse and transcend the boundaries of the language of the dominant culture. Voice has the capacity to make an impact on its surroundings.

> God seems to choose as the agents of change those who are oppressed and most eager to imagine the new.
>
> MDT

Of course, the voice can be used to help others transcend their boundaries and oppression, as well. Dorothee Soelle, a German liberation theologian, accompanied a group of women in Chile who were on a hunger strike to demand information about their abducted husbands, fathers, sons, and brothers. Though she was a woman and a liberationist, she was aware of the limitations of her solidarity with the other women struggling for liberation in Latin America. She says:

> I accepted the invitation with some doubts and reservations. What was the strike all about? The women whose cause I went to endorse slept on mattresses on the stone floor of churches. I stayed in a hotel. Pinned on their clothing were pictures of their husbands, sons, and friends who have disappeared. I went back to my family. Their fight includes physical suffering—I fight only with my typewriter and my voice.[19]

> How do you feel when you have found voice in the face of resistance? It is a whole body thing. You just have to sleep afterwards and rest. Every cell of your body is affected. That's why voice is such a wonderful metaphor; it takes your whole body. There is something profound about the moment. I can't find words for it.
>
> PSR Women

Although worlds apart in life experiences and understandings, Soelle was able to use her voice for the sake of the silenced. She put it to the service of the silenced whose oppressions were not like her own, but who shared in the struggle for liberation. "Voice as resistance" is an expression that reacts to oppressive forces in order to find freedom, be it for oneself or for others with whom a person identifies.

Maria Miguel, a woman in São Paulo, Brazil, lives in a small, one-room structure in a *favela*, a squatter's village. She works in her community as an activist in the land and health movements and participates in women's groups and Bible study. She finds voice through poetry. In describing the effect her poetry has on herself and her community, she says, "Poetry is good for our spirit and our body also. The music and words are a release. They let us breathe freely and give vent to our struggles."[20]

Through voicing the wrongs of society and her passion for change, Maria feels the pulse of liberation through her body and spirit. In the poem, "The People is Poet," she uses the metaphors of mother, warrior, queen, and bird to express the sense of freedom that is within her, and at the same time, the external forces that seek to imprison it. Such a voice resists outside restriction and definition. In this way, the description of Maria Miguel as "a warrior, a rock, a reed for God's voice, giving voice to the people" explains the qualities of a resistant voice and its implications for a theology of preaching that takes liberation seriously.[21]

A resistant voice joins with those of the prophets through the ages calling out for reform, change, and justice. When does the human voice become the locus for God's presence bringing forth transformation?

The Relational Self

In *Women's Ways of Knowing,* the authors point out that the metaphor of voice has been used by many women to describe varying aspects of their personal lives. In describing their lives, women talk about "voice" and "silence," using such phrases as "speaking up," "speaking out," "being silenced," "not being heard," "really listening," "really talking," "words as weapons," "feeling deaf and dumb," "having no words," and "listening to be heard." The endless variety of language reflects the women's sense of mind, self-worth, and feelings of isolation and connection with others. The development of mind, voice, and self are intertwined and inseparable.

This tendency of women to use metaphors of speaking and listening to connote growth is at odds with the use of visual metaphors (equating knowledge with illumination, knowing with seeing, and truth with light) that have been the predominant metaphors of the scientific and philosophical communities. A visual metaphor, such as "the mind's eye," suggests a camera passively recording a static reality. Visual metaphors promote the illusion that disengagement and objectification are central to the construction of knowledge. They encourage standing at a distance. Unlike the eye, however, the ear operates by registering subtle change. The ear, unlike the eye, requires closeness between subject and object. Unlike seeing, speaking and listening suggest dialogue and interaction and, thus, relationship.[22]

This insight coincides with recent scholarship in the field of developmental psychology. In response to theories based on men's experience of autonomous self in relation to others, Carol Gilligan and Jean Baker Miller have researched the development of women. Their conclusions suggest that the highest form of development for women is when the self is brought fully into relationship with others, resulting in honest dialogue. Such dialogue arises from an emerging sense of self-value and self-esteem. It provides space for the self to be affirmed as a worthy partner in conversation. As an important component of the self in dialogue, voice represents the valuing of emerging differences and the full participation of all persons in a conversation that leads to connection and understanding. It is essential to the development of authentic community. In the same way, voice presupposes a social world, the presence of others whom we address and who also respond to us. Voice is central to understanding the relationship of trust, belonging, and intimacy between God and community.

Claiming the Importance of Voice

The use of the metaphor "voice" arises from the recognition of the importance of individuality, self-expression, and truth through relationship. As today's dominant metaphor for power relations between persons and groups in society, "voice" signals the growing cultural acknowledgement of the right to self-expression.

In the essay "Toward an Ethnography of 'Voice' and 'Silence,'" Shulamit Reinharz traces the roots of the metaphor to the historical reality that people with power literally could speak and, at the same time, control the right of others to speak. The powerless were not allowed to speak in the presence of the powerful. Such power relations served to subdue diversity that would threaten the authority of the powerful. For this reason, the history of any group to gain freedom and power in the face of oppression involves a struggle to seize the right to speak and be heard.[23]

The control of power in relationship affects the voice and silence of each group within a system. One in power easily assumes the right to speak. Others are denied that right or must seek permission in order to be heard. In some cases, even when an oppressed voice speaks, especially without the permission of the powerful, that voice is ineffective, because the powerful cannot bear to hear it. Thus, the struggle for voice is not only a struggle to speak, but also a search for an audience to listen.

Because people do not share a single experience of oppression or define themselves in the same way, one person may feel "voiced" in one situation and then "silenced" in another. A person of similar circumstances may feel the opposite. Some persons may feel both "voiced" and "silenced" at the same time. Power relations are complex and subtly nuanced. Nevertheless, when given the opportunity to reflect on their own experience, most persons can easily judge whether they feel "voiced" or "silenced" in a given situation. These are real experiences for human beings that contribute to feelings of belonging with others, on the one hand, and feelings of isolation and fear, on the other.

When oppressed people and groups become acquainted with the metaphor of "voice," they discover a new way to articulate their own experience. By expressing their views and experiences, they affirm their right as distinctive beings to resist objectification and definition by others with the power to define their own realities. Such authority gives them a stronger position in society, increasing their sense of value as persons who have much to contribute to the whole. When this happens, people are free for relationships of mutuality and love.

The emergence of the metaphor of "voice" in our culture marks a new awareness of the possibilities for liberation of the oppressed and true freedom in relation. As such, it pronounces one of the basic themes of the Christian gospel. "Voice" offers a new possibility for understanding the nature of self and world in relation to God and others. It is distinctive. It can call forth authentic selfhood. It is the self's authoritative expression. Sometimes it is resistant, but always it speaks of relationship. It opens the world to new perceptions, new action, and new ways of living. Voice subverts. Voice transforms. As we shall see, the metaphor opens a new possibility for understanding revelation, liberation, memory, longing, and justice. What could be more crucial for the study of preaching!

How shall I break the silence? What word is more eloquent than the silence itself? In the moments before a word is spoken, anything is possible. The empty air is formless void waiting to be addressed.

Barbara Brown Taylor[1]

At Sinai we received both the word and the spirit to understand the word. Some of that original understanding and response of Israel was poured into words, conveyed from mouth to mouth, entrusted in writing, but much of which words were only reflection, remained unsaid, unwritten, a tradition transmitted from soul to soul, inherited like the power to love and kept alive by constant communion with the Word, by studying it, by guarding it, by living it and by being ready to die for it. In the hands of many peoples it becomes a book, in the life of Israel it remained a voice, a Torah within the heart.

Abraham Heschel[2]

If people are not to remain unchanged in suffering, if they are not to be blind and deaf to the pain of others, if they are to move from purely passive endurance to suffering that can humanize them in a productive way, then one of the things they need is language.

Dorothee Soelle[3]

Chapter 2

Created in the Sound of God: Voice in the Old Testament

"Voice" is used by many who long to speak with authority, long to be heard, long to be saved from the forces that have overwhelmed them for centuries. Many of those who use the metaphor of voice, however, fail to realize its deep and significant theological roots. The Jewish and Christian faiths are permeated with strands of tradition that understand God as voice and that depict the human voice as the agent that calls forth God's redemption in the world. Many parts of the Hebrew Bible would be appropriate for study; the subtle nuancings and significances attached to "voice" in the Old Testament vary with different genres, authors, and contexts in which various stories were told and written or edited. Thus there will be no exhaustive accounting of "voice" in the Old Testament here. Simply, however, we will look at the way the understanding of God's voice or "God as voice" is represented in selected texts of the Torah, Writings, and Prophets. Each offers its own intriguing and enlightening understandings of silence and voice in both the human and divine. In each of these, we will search for the theological significance of the emerging metaphor of voice. We will discover the particularities in each of these texts as they relate to both communal and individual voice. We will come to understand that by "finding our voices," we are discovering one aspect of our god-likeness, and that by "claiming voice" we give witness to God's liberating activity.

God's voice...brings a certain peace; is whole and complete; is both familiar and jarring at the same time; rings true; does not have to be filtered; is experienced as intuition; can live in one's memory and be recalled for comfort. *Memphis Theological Seminary Women*

Speaking of Creation—Voice as Agency

We are very familiar with the first verses of Genesis, so familiar that we do not now allow ourselves to be shocked by the voice of God that suddenly intrudes into the void and darkness of the deep.[4] God's Spirit is there, restless and hovering, sweeping over the churning waters. And then, into the chaos come the words, "Let there be light."[5] Words shatter silence, and the great drama of creation begins. The portrait painted of the Creator is as one who speaks.[6] This is God's primary and characteristic action in the story.[7] "Let there be light." With those first words the drama of creation begins to unfold as God speaks into being sky, earth, seas, plant life, the great lights, living creatures of sky and sea, earth, and finally humanity. God authors creation—brings it into being, sometimes ordains its purpose, and gives it a name.[8] Speech demonstrates God's agency and authority in the world. It is one way God makes Godself manifest.

As the creation story finds rhythm, the earth and all things in it, save humanity, are brought into being as five days pass. Slowly, as readers, we begin to realize that through the speaking of God something new is being drawn out of the old. And, at every juncture, the new is pronounced as "good." This teaches us something about God's nature; it is active and draws new, good worlds into being.

We who have been lulled into the predictable repetitions and pattern of the story find ourselves jolted by God's activity on day six. Yes, again something is spoken into being. But this is something, someone created in the image of the creator. This is something, someone in God's likeness. This is humanity. "Let us make humankind in our image..." We wonder how in this story our god-likeness is cast. Perhaps the females and males now brought into being will have God's ability to create new worlds out of the old, to create that which is good, to bring newness out of the chaotic and the restless, and to do this through speech.

Unlike in the first five days, God addresses that which is created.[9] God blesses female and male and speaks to them, giving them power over the world that has now been created. Of all the wonders of creation, God addresses only humans. We know, then, that these creatures have been given the ability to listen. We are left

> Women lose their connection with knowing that they have the power to name something into existence.   *RN*

with the hint of possibility and the hope that they, too, will speak. And we come to suspect that the intimate relationship between God and humanity might well depend upon it.

This creation story, then, in a cursory yet profound way, provides for us the first rendering of God in our canon and sets the stage for our thinking about voice, creation, relationship, authority, agency, god-likeness, and power.

Speaking of Lament and Thanksgiving

The Psalms affirm that God created the world through word. It was by Yahweh's word that the heavens were made, by the breath of Yahweh's mouth.[10] Yahweh spoke and the world came to be.[11] But by far the stronger affirmation made in the Psalms is that the God who speaks is also a God who listens. The humanity that has been created is capable of addressing God.

Many of the songs in the Psalter are laments. The laments are bold; no complaint is out of bounds. Anything, everything is brought to speech as the psalmist names the reality of the world as she knows it and directs her misery, pain, and betrayal to God.[12] In raw and wrenching rhetoric the agony, despair, disease, and oppression is described. Out of the hopelessness comes a cry. "Hear my voice, O god, in my complaint; preserve my life from my dread enemy" (Psalm 64:1). "I call upon you, O Lord; come quickly to me; give ear to my voice when I call on you" (Psalm 141:1).

These lament psalms portray an understanding of a God who is present, who listens, who sustains or delivers. As the reader moves through the graphic portrayal of life and its hardships and injustices, inevitably she arrives at a moment where the assurance that God is a present and listening God moves her to a new place. A new world is drawn out of the old, and in this new world there is hope.[13] This is a movement toward redemption; the movement is initiated by the cry of the human voice, which calls upon God, describes her plight, and asks God to intervene in life. The human voice brings forth the reality of God, for just as clearly as the prophet calls the community to listen to God, the psalmist calls God to listen to the community.

The faithful God does listen. Just as dramatic and evocative as the plea for help is the assurance of the worshiper, then, that God will/has listened. "In my distress I called upon the Lord; to my God. I cried for help. From this temple he heard my voice and my cry to him reached his ears." (Psalm 18:6) "Evening and morning and at noon I utter my complaint and moan; and he will hear my voice" (Psalm 55:17). "I had said in my alarm, 'I am driven far from your sight.' But you heard the voice of my supplications when I cried out to you for help" (Psalm 31:22).

These assurances preserve for us the notion of the resistant human voice that can cry out against injustice, hurt. It is a voice that can offer resistance to enemy and disease, and ultimately even to God. Through resistant speech, the one who cries out is able to move from suffering to assurance that God is still with her. Why? Because her voice has found an audience. *The One who created voice grants it authority.*

This same kind of assurance, the assurance that God is a listening God, is made evident in the penitential psalms where the petitioner is seeking a word of for-giveness. Hope is lodged in her cry. "Lord, hear my voice!" (Psalm 130:1). As in the laments, we witness a transformation, a redemptive movement—a new world is drawn out of the old. The old world of iniquity and confession is replaced by forgiveness from a God of steadfast love and power. (Psalm 130:7) The sinful psalmist waits for Yahweh and, at the same time, pleads with the community of Israel to place hope there also. God, she knows, will hear her cry.

God is trying to get me to grow up, so that I can be in dialogue with God.   *ASU*

There are psalms of lament and penitence. There are also songs of thanksgiving where the worshiper, recalling either deliverance of the community or her own, gives thanks and praise to the God who delivered. Psalm 66 bears witness to both the communal and individual dimensions of gratitude, the first leading, perhaps inevitably, to the second. The communal story is retold. The worshiper recounts the awesome deeds of God who turned the sea into dry land and who eventually brought the community into a new and spacious place. The psalm leads from this recounting of magnificence and power to personal testimony. The worshiper pauses, inviting all to listen. "Now," she says quietly, "let me tell you what this God has done for me." The psalmist is grateful that God has listened (Psalm 66:19). Listening in this psalm relates to covenant, steadfast love, faithfulness, and redemption. *Listening is an active posture of love.*

The psalms bear witness also to the voice of Yahweh. The power of Yahweh, Yahweh's voice, is graphically depicted in Psalm 29. The seven-fold mention of God's voice demonstrates its distinctive strength and might; nothing can compare. Perhaps it had its origin in a song, overheard and borrowed from neighboring Near Eastern communities and transformed into a hymn to the revelation of God.[14] Perhaps the psalmist composed it after witnessing a devastating storm. Regardless of its origin, the psalm witnesses to enormous power. The voice of Yahweh thunders (v. 3), breaks down even the strongest trees (v. 5), flashes forth fire (v. 7), shakes the wilderness (v. 8), causes trees to whirl, strips the forest bare (v. 9). This voice is strong. It is stronger than any force with which it might contend. The voice of God is so strong, it can transform the very landscape of the world in which we live. It is not impotent; it is more powerful than anything.[15] And yet, as Psalm 95 demonstrates, it is also compassionate and tender. The voice of God is like that of the shepherd who cares for the sheep. The psalmist calls the community to listen to that voice (95:7).

Speaking of Deliverance

The story begins with a human cry that rises up to God. God hears the Israelites, who groan under their oppressors, and the great story of deliverance begins to unfold. Moses is keeping watch over sheep. He glimpses the flames of the burning bush.[16] Turning aside to see this strange message, Moses hears a voice calling to him by name and responds, "Here I am." Yahweh speaks to him, comforting, or perhaps warning, that he is standing on holy ground.[17] He is called to bring Yahweh's people out of Egypt. Twice Moses is reminded that Yahweh has heard the people's cry (v. 7, v. 9). The speaker is a *listening* God.

We travel with the Israelites on their journey through the desert. And now, Moses stands in the wilderness on the east side of the Jordan River. He and the Israelites have, at long last, completed their grueling and circuitous journey. They stand looking at the land they have sought for decades. Moses, knowing that he will not be allowed to make that final step into the land of the Canaanites, stands to speak to the community just as Yahweh has instructed. One can imagine the exhilaration and sadness with which Moses brought forth this farewell address. There must have been so much he wanted to say to this people; there would be so much he would want them to remember. He would want them to recall how God had been with them on the journey. He would want them to remember how they were to go about being God's people in a new and foreign land. He would want them to renew the covenant they had made with God; he would want them to be faithful. Cast as his last words to the thronging crowds standing before him, Deuteronomy brings us the words of his farewell.[18]

Formative to the book of Deuteronomy and serving as a prelude to the expositions, the reinterpretations and amplifications on the Law, is the careful and detailed accounting of the experience of the Israelites at Mount Horeb (see Deutermony 4). Moses calls upon the community to remember the experience of standing at the foot of the mountain. Moses describes the blazing of the fire up to the heavens and the dark clouds. He recalls for them that, at that moment, Yahweh spoke to them. "You approached and stood at the foot of the mountain while the mountain was blazing up to the very heavens, shrouded in dark clouds. Then the LORD spoke to you out of the fire. You heard the sound [voice] of words but saw no form; **there was only a voice** [emphasis ours]. He declared to you his covenant." The voice spoke to them the commandments, the laws, by which they should live.

This rendering of the story of the giving of the Law raises fascinating questions. What does it mean that God, in this story, is only voice? In this story, the Law is given, not through writing, but through speech. The laws were written on the tablets of stone only after the people had first heard them. The voice of God was so frightening that the people thought that to hear it might mean they would die. What does this rhetorical relationship between God and God's people mean for the way they live out their callings? Why is this story so important and fundamental that it is revisited in chapter 5? "Hear, O Israel, the statutes and ordinances that I am addressing to you today; you shall learn them and observe them diligently. The LORD our God made a covenant with us at Horeb. Not with our ancestors did the LORD make this covenant, but with us, who are all of us here alive today. The LORD spoke with you face to face at the mountain, out of the fire. At that time I was standing between the LORD and you to declare to you the words of the LORD; for you were afraid because of the fire and did not go up to the mountain" (Deuteronomy 5:1–5).

Almost exclusively in Old Testament narrative, God's voice is heard by individuals, those who are then called to bring the word that was heard to others.[19] Not so in Deuteronomy. Just as in Genesis the spoken word of God brought about creation, here the spoken word forms the covenant community. Though the people are afraid and ask that Moses listen for them, initially they hear as one the word that Yahweh has spoken. The spoken word demanded and defined covenant. Even the casual reader of the book of Deuteronomy will realize that "hearing" is of fundamental importance to the Israelite faith. The *Shema* in Deuteronomy 6 forcefully expounds one of the central tenets of faithfulness: "Hear, O Israel: The LORD is our God, the LORD alone. You shall love the LORD your God with all your heart, and with all your soul, and with all your might. Keep these words." The admonition, or invitation, to hear provides the prelude to the listing of the Ten Commandments: "Hear, O Israel, the statutes and ordinances that I am addressing to you today; you shall learn them and observe them diligently. The LORD our God made a covenant with us at Horeb."[20]

When we return to the experience at Mount Horeb in Deuteronomy 5, the emphasis is on the contemporary nature of the covenant. The hermeneutical formula within the story emphasizes the present nature of covenant relationship. As Moses retells the story, he remembers the voice of God as it spoke in the past, but he retells the story so that the hearers can realize that the covenant is of the now. Note these words "with us, we, these ones, here today, all of us living." The text uses seven words, one used immediately after the other (5:3), to stress the contemporary claims of the covenant upon the lives of those listening.[21] When God is rendered as "voice" the remembering of the story in Deuteronomy is not a longing for the past; rather, the remembering is a reminder that God is capable of speaking to each and every generation—and does, in order to sustain the life of the covenant claims.[22] Voice was an indication to the community that God was living, that God was still dynamically present with them even as they prepared for their new venture. Voice was indicative of a God in relationship.

The living quality of the spoken word is evident in Deuteronomy when Moses recounts for the Israelites the memories of Horeb. He says to them: "Then the LORD spoke to you out of the fire. You heard the voice of the words but saw no form; there was only a voice" (4:12). The "voice of the word" is its sound, its activity, its embodiment, its agency, and its life.[23] The fire accompanying the word signals holiness and power.

Throughout its history, Israel understood itself to be a "called people." Yahweh was a God who spoke and the Israelites were a people called to hear. Though two distinct traditions can be observed, one where God appeared to eye and one to ear, to be "face to face" or "mouth to mouth" in the Old Testament is to experience intimate disclosure. To hear is truly to be in the presence of. When the people heard all the words that Yahweh had spoken, they answered in one voice (Exodus 24:3–6, 8). Addressed by God, they were moved to speech.

The word, the covenant, can be made present in a particular time and place because God is of the essence of voice. Through the human voice, memory of divine voice is kept alive. Efforts to preserve the words of God at Horeb were not because of the sacredness of the record, but because of the sacredness of the event in which God through speech disclosed meaning. The hope was that the word event could be repeated. The voice would form community anew.

This longing to live in the presence of a speaking God moved the Israelites to construct the tent of meeting in the wilderness as they journeyed from Egypt to Canaan.[24] Once God had spoken to the Israelites revealing the Law, the tent was constructed. The tent was the locus of God's speaking presence. Through voice, there was a disclosure of God's purpose. It was a meeting place—not a monument to God, but the place that could be filled with the presence of God in dialogue with humanity. This tent provided Moses with privacy and isolation for a conversation with God. In its darkness, there were experienced the moments when Yahweh and Moses spoke "face to face" (Exodus 33:11) or as in Numbers 12:8, (KJV) "mouth to mouth." To those who stood outside, the presence of God was made manifest by the descent of the pillar of cloud. *There is a difference between seeing and hearing, however.* Moses would chat with God, much like a person would chat with a friend. This is a relational God, a living presence with Israel on its journey.[25]

For the Deuteronomist, it is important that the people continue to live with an ear toward the "voice" of God. Thus, the constant refrain commands them to "hear the voice." This phrase is most often translated "obey the voice." While the words "obey" and "hear" are related etymologically in several cultures, to translate *shema* simply as "obey" misses the element of mutuality that is present between humanity and this speaking God. It is more helpful perhaps to consider this phrase an invitation for the Hebrew people to stay in the presence of the God who once spoke from the top of the mountain. When God is understood as voice, revelation is mutual. It is an event in which there is both giving and receiving. Divine/human dialogue with questions and answers, objections and counterstatements, give and take, interacting tension between God and person is characteristic of this theophany. Because revelation occurs through voice, there is the giving of that which is revealed and the receiving of that which is perceived. Relationship is established. To "hear the voice" is to stay in covenant, stay present to, stay "face-to-face" with God.

This Jewish legend illustrates the listening and speaking dynamic of contemporary covenant.

The Baal Shem Tov raised the questions: What is the purpose of the voice? If no one ever hears it, of what avail is it? If there is always

> Voice as a primary metaphor for God? This does not ring true for me. I agree that we have the power, like God, to speak new worlds into being. But I find in my own cultural context, the Asian community, that there is so much communicated that is not spoken. Silence is valued highly. So much is said through silence. Maybe that, too, is voice.   COD

one who hears it, would he presume to admit it? And would anybody believe him? The Baal Shem Tov explained:

> The voice that goes forth from above does not reach the physical ear of man. There is no speech, there are not words, the voice is not heard. It is uttered not in sounds but in thoughts, in signs that man must learn to perceive. All the longings to return to God that come to man as well as all his inner awakenings of either joy or fear are due to that voice. Hear, O Israel. Every day a voice goes out of Mount Horeb, which the righteous men perceive. Hear, O Israel, means hear the voice that proclaims all the time, at every moment. Every day he who is worthy receives the Torah standing at Sinai, he hears the Torah from the mouth of the Lord as Israel did when they stood at Sinai. Every Israelite is able to attain this level, the level of standing at Sinai.[26]

The account in Deuteronomy of the wilderness wanderings and the remembering of the moments when God's voice was heard provides a model of ongoing interpretation and reflection on past tradition that keeps the tradition alive and adaptable.[27] It is a model for preaching. *The human voice contextualizes the word.* Deuteronomy itself is cast as Moses' interpretation (proclamation) of the past event at Mount Horeb. Moses speaks of the importance of the historic event to the present community—a community not standing at the foot of the mountain but, now, at the edge of the river. In addition, the story is told by a theologian(s) centuries later who is trying to make clear the implications of the story for his particular and present community. Subsequently, we read the story and through our own distinctive voices speak of the story's importance to our own contemporary community. God's word is dependent upon the human voice to contextualize it for the present. The word is not static and confined; it is rich and multivalent. It calls forth a multitude of voices in different generations to embody it and give it life.

That is why, no doubt, as the Israelites begin to make their way into the land of Canaan knowing that Moses will not be with them, he brings to them a word of comfort for their futures. Yahweh, Moses tells them (Deuteronomy 18:15–22), will raise up a prophet for them. The prophet will be one who will listen to God and who will report the words of God to them. This is, he reminds them, what they requested at Horeb, fearing that to hear the voice of God would bring death. Yahweh promises that the tradition of the prophet among them will go on. Yahweh promises that Yahweh will put words into the prophet's mouth, and the prophet will speak as Yahweh commands. This text is about word and words (see vv. 18, 19, 20, 21). Prophets continue to be called by voice to give voice to the word of God for God's people.

Speaking a Prophetic Word

Young Samuel in the temple hears a voice calling out to him. The voice is not recognizable because Samuel does not yet know Yahweh, but with the insight and help of a spiritual guide, the blinded and aging Eli, Samuel comes to know Yahweh as a god who speaks.

Elijah stands at the top of Mount Carmel with 450 prophets of Baal and 400 prophets of Asherah. The prophets call upon the name of Baal. They cry out to Baal, "Answer us." There is no answer; there is no voice. Voice is the distinction in this story between the true and false god.[28] Elijah then, after hearing the sound of sheer silence from the cave, hears the voice of Yahweh, plain and articulate, pronouncing a word of prophetic mission.

These and other intriguing stories about God and voice serve as prelude to the latter prophets, the writing prophets, whose written words are said to be uttered for God to the community. One of these is Jeremiah.

That Jeremiah is about silence and voice is easily demonstrated by the overwhelming number of references to the words *speak, proclaim, cry out, voice, word, listen, hear, ears, say, call,* and *mouth* as the words from God through Jeremiah are delivered to the community. This book provides us with an extensive collection of the edited word of the prophet and intimate glimpses into his personal life.[29]

We are alerted in Jeremiah 1:2 that the word of Yahweh comes directly to this one named Jeremiah, son of Hilkiah. It comes during a particular time in history, first in the days of King Josiah, and then later in the days of King Jehoakim and King Zedekiah of Judah. Indeed, the word of Yahweh came until the community went into exile. The editor of this book isn't concerned with some of our most pressing and penetrating questions: What is the relationship between God's word and the voice of this prophet? Can the human voice reflect divine reality? Simply, the word comes. Just as Isaiah hears the voice of Yahweh crying, "Whom shall I send?" (6:8), so Ezekiel and Jeremiah are visited by the "word of Yahweh" that finds them and speaks to them. The word is active. It is spoken. It is spirit and sound. This word calls Jeremiah to a vocation of listening and speaking.

From the very moment of Jeremiah's conception, he has been formed and fashioned with both the ability and call to speak. He has been known, consecrated, and appointed by Yahweh to be a prophet. Jeremiah knows that this call is a call to speak; he protests that he does not know how. The call persists, however. He is to go where sent and speak what is commanded. Yahweh's presence will go with him.

In an intimate moment of ordination, Yahweh reaches forth with Yahweh's hand and touches Jeremiah's mouth. Yahweh's voice is the breath, the spirit that comes upon the prophet and utters the commission: Jeremiah is to pluck up, pull down, destroy, and overthrow. He is to do all these things with speech; the spoken word is powerful enough to destroy what in God's world needs to be destroyed. And yet, that is not all. Jeremiah is also to build and plant; something new is to be drawn forth from the old. This call narrative is an intimate relational portrait of God and person. It is the portrait of a God who is restlessly, constantly intervening in the world to move human life forward.

> I heard my call as a voice in my spirit. Even now, for preaching, I often hear that voice in my spirit that speaks. God is still speaking. *SLK*

"Thus says Yahweh." "Thus says Yahweh." "Thus says Yahweh." The repetition of this phrase reminds the reader of Jeremiah that (1) Yahweh speaks and (2) that Yahweh speaks a word addressed to a particular context, time and place. The one speaking is designated by a variety of names (the LORD, the LORD God of hosts, LORD of hosts, LORD God of Israel, the LORD who made the earth, the Lord of you,

> It's a hard thing to claim, the role of the prophet. I don't think of myself as one, but it is what I want to be. It is scary. It is delicate. Sometimes it is beyond me. *COD*

the LORD of Hosts, God of Israel). Each name simultaneously designates the one from whom the message comes and provides the locus of authority for the hearer. A less formal phrase, *says the LORD,* is often inserted into the individual units, as a constant reminder for the listener/reader that God is the author of what is spoken.[30]

Is this prophet, then, a passive recipient or a recording instrument for the God who has called him? No. Neither is he a person who acquires his voice by his own strength and labor. He is an active partner in the event. His response to what is disclosed to him turns revelation into dialogue. "Revelation does not happen when God is alone."[31]

As Jeremiah responds with mind and heart to the word that is given him, his own grief and despair become part of that which is spoken and remembered. His own suffering becomes entangled with God's. In 8:18—9:1, the anger of Yahweh and the despair of the community bring uncontrollable grief to the prophet, who loves both. He hears the cry of the people from across the land. He also hears the cry of Yahweh, who cannot understand why the people have continued to provoke anger. The prophet stands between them. The cries are deafening. His joy is gone. His heart is sick. The hurt of the people has become his own (v. 21).

It is difficult to determine clearly the beginnings and endings to units in chapter 8. It is difficult to determine who is speaking and who is listening. This confusion underscores the profound and immense emotional experience as grief blurs sound. Boundaries become unclear. Speech comes spontaneously. In times of lament there are often uncontrollable outpourings of grief. As one speech ends, or even before, another begins, so that sounds blend. There is a constant roar of weeping and wailing. The laments of the prophet and God become indistinguishable; they are now one.[32]

Jeremiah brings a word of condemnation to the community; he describes their waywardness. In Jeremiah 3:21–25 a voice of despair is heard. It is a plaintive voice, and it is the voice of Israel's children. Those who have forgotten their God are crying out, and God is calling for the faithless to return and be healed. The call to return is answered by the children who come to Yahweh. They realize that they have been deluded, and the root of their sin is that they have not heard the "voice of Yahweh their God." Out of their not hearing God's voice comes their own despair.

As we would expect in Jeremiah, the Deuteronomistic refrain to "hear the voice" and "hear the word" finds a rightful place in the prophet's message. "Only acknowledge your guilt…you have not obeyed [heard] my voice, says the Lord" (Jeremiah 3:13). "And when I spoke to you persistently, you did not listen, and when I called you, you did not answer" (Jeremiah 7:13). "Because all of you sinned against the LORD and did not obey [hear] his voice" (Jeremiah 40:3).

Thus, God and the prophet call the community again and again to hear the voice: "But this command I gave them, 'Obey [Hear] my voice, and I will be your God, and you shall be my people'" (Jeremiah 7:23). "Now therefore amend your ways and your doings, and obey [hear] the voice of the LORD your God, and the LORD will change his mind about the disaster that he has pronounced against you" (Jeremiah 26:13). "Just obey [hear] the voice of the LORD in what I say to you, and it shall go well with you, and your life shall be spared" (Jeremiah 38:20).

This prophetic book of Jeremiah is about voice and its hearing. It is also about silence. These are foundational to life and death, covenant, and redemption. The interplay of voice and silence, and of hearing, are woven intricately through the volume as

- God speaks
- The community fails to listen and to voice their despair
- God, however, calls a prophet to speak
- The prophet speaks
- The people do not listen
- Later, the people go into exile
- God's voice finds them there and brings a word of hope

It is not easy, of course, to listen and discern God's voice among all the others that compete for and demand our attention. In Jeremiah 27, God acknowledges that these voices are present in our world and at the same time, through stringent repetition, implores the people not to heed them. "You, therefore, must not listen to your prophets, your diviners, your dreamers, your soothsayers, or your sorcerers…Do not listen to the words of the prophets who are telling you not to serve the king of Babylon …I have not sent them. Do not listen to the words of your prophets who are prophesying to you, saying, 'The vessels of the Lord's house will soon be brought back from Babylon,' for they are prophesying a lie to you. Do not listen to them: serve the king of Babylon and live."

The word that the prophet Jeremiah is called to speak is, unlike those of the false prophets, a resistant word. It is a word which is intended to evoke a different consciousness, usher in a new order among the people, challenge the way of life that they have come to know, a way that is comfortable to the dominant and to the strong.

The gay and lesbian communities are today's prophets. They ask, "Is Christianity just an exclusive club, or is it for everybody?"   AS

The temple sermon in Jeremiah 7 portrays this resistant word. The word calls for reexamination and change. Verse 5 calls for the community to amend their ways, act justly, not to oppress the widow, or shed innocent blood, not to go after other gods. These words offer an alternative, undoubtedly, to the customary day-to-day life. The people are unaware that their behavior has become "ungodlike," contrary to the covenantal relationship. Jeremiah is called to bring not only general indictments to the community, but outlines as well the particular and specific transgressions. In the end, Jeremiah is told that he will speak these harsh words, but the people will not listen. When he calls, they will not answer. Again, the story is about speaking and listening—the people did not listen, although God spoke persistently (v. 13); they did not hear or incline their ear (v. 24); they did not listen (v. 25). In the end, Jeremiah will say that this is the nation that did not hear the voice of Yahweh their God.

"Whether a low voice or loud and clear, anonymously or publicly by word or by action, by diminution or announcing hope, the prophetic witness is costly."[33] There is no more graphic portrayal of the forces that seek to silence a spokesperson for God than that provided by the narrative account of the prophet Jeremiah. Consecrated even before conception, called as a child, the account of Jeremiah's ministry is a chilling reminder that forces are at work that attempt to muffle the sound, if not completely silence his voice. The reader of the account is not misled; from its beginning we are told that the task this young man is called to perform will not be easy. We hold no illusions: kings, princes, priests, all of the higher authorities, indeed all the people, will fight against him. Jeremiah is promised Yahweh's presence; Jeremiah is promised that he will prevail. So Jeremiah speaks—a costly action.

Could this prophet have known the resistance that would meet his word? Could he have anticipated all that the world would do to try to silence message and messenger? Why is the prophetic voice so dangerous that it needs to be silenced?

Through graphic metaphor, informed by frustration and pain, Jeremiah describes for us his ongoing experience of being the spokesperson for God's word. Though the words were first a joy and a delight, he finds that the community is not receptive to that which he speaks. The people plot against him, and Jeremiah offers complaint to Yahweh. In his frustration, he calls out for revenge against those who will not hear and who actively oppose him.

Jeremiah suffers active resistance. He is struck, put in stocks. He feels that Yahweh has enticed him and seduced him into bringing words that, in turn, bring him reproach and derision. Yet, the "fire in his bones" will not allow him the safety of silence. In the end, he sits in his prison cell where he waits. Lowered

> That's why people work hard to stifle voice. It isn't containable. We can't just automatically have it under our control. Therefore, it becomes a threat. The idea that there's something within us that guides and directs puts some people off balance.
>
> *RN*

into the cistern, he sinks into the mire. Throughout his ministry he feels like the lamb led to slaughter; he is the laughingstock. The word has become a burden. And in his despair, he cries out to God to be healed and saved. "See how they say to me: Where is the word? Let it come."

Echoes

God speaking creation into existence, God listening to the anguish and lamentation of the community, God speaking to the community and covenant forming, God calling the prophet to speak a word that will bring the community to justice: together these paint a portrait of a God in relationship with the people. The relationship is dynamic, changing, challenging. It never crystallizes; it is never static. This listening/speaking God offers again and again the possibility of the new that surpasses the old; this God stands ready to draw it forth. If only the people will stay close enough to hear the whispers.[34] If only they will be strong and wise enough to choose life.

Voice is the agency of the living God. It is a dynamic spiritual force that makes covenant and calls us to new life. Through voice and the act of speaking, God calls a people into existence. Nothing in the world of things can satisfy the fundamental hunger in the human spirit for the voice and presence of the living God.

But here we encounter a paradox, a dynamic tension at the heart of the human-divine reality. God creates, calls, and pursues; we fail to believe, refuse to listen, and fall into a despair from which only God can rescue. God calls and reaches, humankind withholds or rejects. This happens as God calls us out of the chaotic, creates new possibilities, and draws us beyond ourselves into something new and glorious. In this way God, through speech, discloses new meaning and becomes a living presence on our journey—even when we fail to be hearing people.

The journey that marks the life of the prophet is more complex than this. The prophet is wrapped up, restless in, and wrestling with God's word, like the prophet Jeremiah. The realities from which we are never free are paired: joy and burden, acceptance and rejection, compliment and complaint, trust and betrayal, hope and despair, laughter and lament, companionship and loneliness. The voice that speaks for God must speak to these paired realities that mark the human-divine experience. The only assurance the prophet has is that the faithful God, even in divine silence, hears and is moved by our human cry. To hear the voice, then, is to stay in covenant. Listen and hear the voice of God.

In our own lives the voice of God speaks slowly, a syllable at a time. Reaching the peak of years, dispelling some of our intimate illusions and learning how to spell the meaning of life experiences backwards, some of us discover the scattered syllables form a single phrase.

Abraham Heschel[1]

...scripture as language consists of human words and only human words. As such they are limited and require interpretation, just as all human language does. But this human word, as we will see, is the symbolic locus of divine revelation.

Sandra Schneiders[2]

Chapter 3

The Power to Speak:
Voice in the New Testament

Can human speech reflect divine reality? The New Testament witness responds to this question with a resounding "Yes!" Listening for the presence of "voice" throughout the gospel narrative allows certain dimensions of the story to emerge with new significance. Especially in the story related by the author of Luke-Acts, the presence of God's Spirit sparks conversation that is truthful and liberating among the most ordinary of human beings. The unmistakable mark of the Spirit's presence with people is prophetic speech.

Although "speech" stories are found in all the gospel accounts, scholars have argued that the theology of Luke-Acts reflects a greater sense of continuity with Jewish understandings of the work of the Holy Spirit in relation to prophetic speech.[3] Luke-Acts demonstrates most fully the importance of the human voice in the divine realm through the story of Jesus' and his followers' empowerment for proclamation. The most significant stories relating to the manifestation of "voice" within the narrative of Luke-Acts build on a strong tradition within Hebrew scriptures to reinforce an inclusive theology of "voice" for proclamation.

Speaking of New Beginnings

The Luke-Acts narrative begins with a profound reversal of the "voiced" and the "silenced." As the curtain opens, we are introduced to Zechariah and Elizabeth, two good people living in shame because they had no children. Zechariah was a priest, and his wife a descendant of Aaron.

As a priest, Zechariah was one of eight hundred men in the division of Abijah. The odds of being chosen to burn incense before God in the Holy of Holies on behalf of the entire assembly would have been slim, a once-in-a-lifetime experience for an average priest. To offer sacrifice and pronounce the priestly benediction would have been nothing less than an occasion of profound honor for Zechariah.[4]

The action of the story begins as Zechariah enters into the sanctuary of God and finds himself in the company of a stranger, standing to the right of the altar, speaking directly to him. This unexpected intrusion in such a place of mystery terrified him, so that he responded defensively to the favorable news that was offered by the messenger. The stranger spoke of future possibilities; Zechariah could only think of the present reality. The stranger announced the birth of a child who would be filled with prophetic power in a "prophetless" age. Zechariah refused to entertain fantasies of new life coming to people of old age, even though the story of Abraham and Sarah was embedded deeply in his memory. Just as Sarah laughed at the pronouncement of strangers that she would give birth at such a late date, Zechariah mirrored the same disbelief, even though he knew of Sarah's sure delivery of Isaac.

The consequences of disbelief are extreme in Luke's gospel. In this story, Zechariah lost voice entirely. The priest of the people, with the authority and social standing that allowed him to make public proclamation, stood speechless before the assembly, only able to attempt meaningful gestures to people who were expecting words. The representative of the male religious establishment was silenced.

Stunned and speechless, Zechariah went home to his wife who, for years, had lived a speechless existence. Elizabeth was considered unworthy to speak on two counts. As a woman, Elizabeth was silenced by a society that would not permit her to speak in public. As a childless woman, Elizabeth was shamed into silence by a community that sanctioned motherhood as the primary source of honor for her.[5] Perhaps Zechariah's sudden silence allowed him to embrace Elizabeth with a fresh love arising from a new respect. They now shared a mutual understanding and need. Soon after Zechariah's loss of voice, Elizabeth became pregnant.

This event is followed in Luke's gospel by a similar story of visitation by a stranger. This time the stranger appeared, not in the temple, but in a house located in the small town of Nazareth in Galilee. The stranger spoke to a woman named Mary, rather than a priest. Instead of responding in fear to the stranger's pronouncement, the young woman was puzzled. The stranger explained that the outpouring of the Holy Spirit on her would make possible the birth of a child that would be the Messiah of God. In contrast to Zechariah, Mary accepted the possibility of the stranger's message for her life and acted on it.

Ignoring the social convention that considered women too vulnerable to travel alone, Mary quickly set out on a journey from Nazareth to the hill country for a meaningful conversation with Elizabeth, her cousin.[6] Confirmation of the stranger's message awaited her in Elizabeth. Elizabeth was indeed pregnant, and she spoke with prophetic power of Mary's role in God's unfolding plan. This was a sure sign of the Spirit's presence with her.

Luke records a beautiful hymn, commonly known as the Magnificat, as Mary's response to Elizabeth's words. The speech is confident and bold in its prophetic tone. Like Hannah's before her, Mary's words echo the language of the ancient prophets with eloquence and power. Her words reflect attention to her own private and personal experience with God, a characteristic of women's speech.[7] Although her speech takes place within the privacy of Elizabeth's home, it is recorded for public memory and embraced by the Christian community as a manifestation of the power of God's presence.[8] Reminiscent of the midwives of Egypt who, in private, subverted the royal decree to kill the Israelite boys, the voices of Elizabeth and Mary ring with midwifery qualities that assist the arrival of God's new realm.[9]

When Elizabeth gave birth to the promised child, Zechariah's speech was not immediately restored. The community had refused to accept Elizabeth's naming of the child.[10] Only after Zechariah confirmed Elizabeth's authoritative pronouncement in writing was his speech restored. The naming of "John" by Zechariah suggests his acceptance of the reality of God made known by the stranger before his child's conception and his willingness to assist in the fulfillment of God's plan through this child. It also validates before the community the truth of Elizabeth's words that God had authorized her to speak.

Not only did Zechariah recover his voice, but his speech took on a prophetic quality that reflected the fresh revelation of the power of the God's Spirit.[11] This speech not only honors God as the source of Zechariah's strength and good fortune but also restores Zechariah's honor as a public speaker.

Thus, Luke's Gospel opens with a figure of authority who is shamed into silence and two silent women who are inspired to speak with authority.

Zechariah's voice is restored only after he experiences the shame of his own voicelessness and comes to trust the authority of other unlikely persons who give voice to reality.

After the stories of Jesus' birth, Luke records a scene in which Mary and Joseph presented their child at the temple. The man Simeon and the woman Anna, both of considerable age, began to speak with a truth and power that reflected the arrival of God's realm. Consistent with a social world that valued the words of men more than the words of women, Simeon's speech was recorded, whereas Anna's was lost.[12]

The time of preparation comes to a close in Luke's Gospel through the preaching of John the Baptist, the son of Zechariah and Elizabeth. This took place in an era when some scholars had declared that prophecy, through the inspiration of the Holy Spirit, had ceased. They believed that only the echo of Spirit was now given to provide wisdom and understanding for students of the Torah, rather than the bestowing of the full presence of the Holy Spirit for an inspired, prophetic word.[13] The person and words of John the Baptist contradicted this claim, however. The presence of the Spirit was manifested in the prophetic voice of John announcing the coming of God's realm.

As Luke's story unfolds, the arrival of God's presence in the person and ministry of Jesus is first a story about faithful people coming to speech. The most likely spokesperson for the arrival of God's reign is silenced. The least likely people are given voice to announce the presence of God's new activity in the world. God's power is made known through ordinary people finding "voice."

Speaking of the New Ordered Realm of God

In Luke's Gospel, the person Jesus takes center stage at the time of his baptism. The baptism of John for forgiveness of sins was understood to symbolize a radical break with the old establishment and a dramatic entrance into a new realm of God. For Jesus, baptism marked his passage into ministry as the representative of God's new order.

According to the Jewish tradition, the correct ordering of time, place, and behavior was considered a way for human beings to participate in divine reality. The established leaders in Jesus' day promoted an order that was centered in Sabbath laws (time), temple cult (place), and purity codes defining all kinds of relationships (behavior). Human speech was governed closely by these rules, as well. The new order of God, announced by both John the Baptist and Jesus, radically redefined time, place and behavior, and thus speech, in relation to God.[14]

Luke records Jesus stepping into this anticipated realm and beginning to pray. Perhaps this action signified Jesus' radical allegiance to God alone. As he was praying, the Holy Spirit descended upon Jesus in a visible way, anointing him to speak the prophetic word. The Spirit was accompanied by the voice of God. Speaking directly to Jesus, the voice said, "You are my Son, the Beloved, with you I am well pleased" (Luke 3:22). The voice of God confirmed the identity of Jesus as representative of God's new order, a ministry empowered by the presence of the Spirit. God's favor came to rest within the voice of the prophet.

Although arguments have been made for a theology of "adoption" [15] at work in this passage, some scholars suggest that Luke presents Jesus' baptism and receiving of the Holy Spirit as directly corresponding to the descent of the Holy Spirit at Pentecost. [16] As such, the Spirit's presence gives Jesus the power to speak with authority. This authority is demonstrated in the two subsequent stories in the unfolding narrative: Jesus' encounter with the Deceiver in the wilderness and the clash with his home congregation in Nazareth.

The Spirit drove Jesus away from the crowds and into the wilderness to be tested. Perhaps this implies that a separation from other voices and a journey into solitude could be an important step in the process of discovering voice in relation to ministry. Here in the wilderness Jesus encountered a persuasive, but deceptive voice. Tough challenges called forth Jesus' most powerful voice.

In this story, suggestions by the Deceiver were strategically offered to Jesus to entice him into exercising various kinds of power that were different from prophetic speech in order to manifest the realm of God on earth. Turning stones to bread would be a small, but powerful act—something that would fulfill the people's expectations of a Messiah who could usher in material prosperity for Israel. The Deceiver's second offer of political rule would require Jesus to command armies and order governments as one sent by God to gain political freedom for his people from the Roman Empire. The third temptation to defy earthly limitations would have confirmed Jesus' status as the heavenly authority but would have called for God's exercise of supernatural power over the universe. The Human One, the prophet of God's truth, comes to exercise the power of prophetic speech, however. To each temptation, Jesus responds with a word from the tradition of the prophets that silences the opposition. In each instance, Jesus' identity is confirmed by what he speaks. His response to the Deceiver verifies the truth of God's claim on Jesus as one who speaks for God.

The stories of Jesus' baptism and temptation ultimately lead to a narrative that reveals his prophetic mission. At his home synagogue in Nazareth, Jesus delivers his first sermon, an event that clearly defines the shape of his future ministry.

First, Jesus read from the Prophets. The passage that we know as Isaiah 61 has been modified in Luke's Gospel to emphasize liberation as the primary goal of Jesus' prophetic ministry. It speaks of the anointing of the prophet by God for the purpose of *proclaiming* good news, release, sight, freedom, and Jubilee. Isaiah's words place the ministry of Jesus squarely in the line of the prophets. [17]

Second, Jesus sat down and said, "Today this scripture has been fulfilled in your hearing." Reality was changed when the words of the ancient prophet were spoken by the voice of the contemporary preacher. As Jesus claimed these words and embodied them within his voice, the future possibility held by them was transformed into a present reality among the hearers.

Third, Jesus declared, "Truly I tell you, no prophet is accepted in the prophet's hometown." His statement was not typical of a preacher's reaction to a positive response to a sermon. Apparently the congregation had assumed a self-congratulatory posture, an attitude of pride that one of their own would be chosen by God for this ambitious task. To them, Jesus' words seemed to imply that God was looking upon them with some sort of special favor. Jesus acknowledged, however, the challenge of getting those closest to him to hear and understand. He realized that the hometown folk failed to discern the full import of his announcement of liberty for the oppressed.

Finally, when Jesus clarified his sermon for them, explaining that God had worked through prophets before for the benefit of those outside the Jewish tradition, they rejected him. As long as they thought that Jesus' ministry was for their own personal benefit, they were receptive. When they heard that God's liberation was directed toward persons outside the periphery of their own social order, they rejected Jesus. Liberation could be tolerated only within the confines of the established order of their world. They refused to imagine that a new order of reality could be God's plan of liberation for them if that world included persons unlike themselves.

According to Luke's Gospel, Jesus' authority to speak God's new order was established at the beginning of Jesus' ministry. The Spirit that empowered Jesus to speak prepared him for the task. Through separation and testing, Jesus established his own prophetic voice. Thus, he was able to maintain authority in the face of misunderstanding and rejection by those closest to him. Jesus' authority demonstrated both Spiritual power and liberation—signs of the new ordered realm of God.

Speaking of the Unfolding Ministry of Jesus

References to "voice" and "speaking" continue to arise throughout Luke's Gospel. The following section discusses texts where "voice" is heard in ways that are particularly intriguing for this study.

Among the voices heard in Luke are those of demons. Soon after the story of Jesus' opening sermon in Nazareth, the author places Jesus in a situation where he is confronted twice by persons possessed by demonic spirits (Luke 4:33–37; 41). In both cases, the demons were quick to acknowledge Jesus as the one sent by God to usher in the new order. The demons recognized the voice of God's authority, but these voices were threatened by the radical transformation that Jesus announced.

Later in the same gospel, Jesus is confronted again with a man possessed by multiple demons whose name was "Legion" (Luke 8:26–39). Again, the demons responded in fear. Although they recognized Jesus' true identity when his own community did not, Jesus silenced the demons and exorcised them from the helpless victim. They had strong voices, but they were subduing the true voice of the individuals they possessed. The demonic voices held human beings hostage. God's new order demanded that persons be set free from outside forces that presumed to speak for them.

> In thinking about demonic voices that intend to destroy or diminish others, a question arises: Is the act of bringing a life-giving voice a way of silencing the other voice? I don't know if it is necessarily quieting the other, as much as it is the voicing of the alternative. A re-framing.
>
> COD

Another interesting text in Luke tells the story of Jesus' encounter with the widow of Nain (Luke 7:11–17). This widow's only son had just died, leaving her in a state of extreme vulnerability. Sons and mothers were closely bonded, and the son was responsible for the economic security of his mother as long as he was alive. Without her son, this woman was destitute and completely dependent upon the favor of her community. By raising the man from death, Jesus was restoring life to the widow as well as to the son.[18] This action of Jesus parallels the story found in 1 Kings 17 of Elijah raising the widow's son, alluding to Jesus' prophetic power as the source of this action.[19] The interesting detail of the story for our purposes, however, is that, at the pivotal point of restoration, the son sat up and began speaking in response to Jesus' command.

The person was brought to speech as the fullest expression of his life restored.[20]

In another familiar story, Jesus is welcomed into the home of Martha (Luke 10:38–42). Her sister Mary took the posture of a student, joining the other disciples in learning from the teacher. Although women of that culture were not permitted to study with men, Jesus affirms the action of Mary as appropriate and important. He is honored that she has recognized the significance of his voice.

Luke's story of the transfiguration of Jesus (Luke 9:28–36) gives added confirmation to Jesus' prophetic power. As in the story of his baptism, Jesus experiences the power of spiritual transformation while he is praying, and the voice of God is heard confirming the authority of Jesus as the spokesperson for God. The mountain in this story further alludes to Old Testament accounts of God's communication with prophets. Here Jesus is joined by Moses and Elijah, who represent the presence of God through law (Exodus 24:12–18) and the prophets (1 Kings 17:24). In conversation together, they discuss Jesus' approaching "exodus." The cloud and the voice confirm the identity of Jesus as the "interpreter and fulfillment" of what had already been spoken by God through the Law and the prophets.[21] The voice instructs the followers *to listen to the voice* of Jesus.[22]

In Luke's account of the triumphal entry into Jerusalem, the Pharisees speak to Jesus from the crowd, requesting Jesus to silence the disciples' loud praise. Jesus replies cryptically, "I tell you, if these were silent, the stones would shout out." Interpreters have pondered the meaning of this phrase. Some suggest that it refers to the involvement of all creation in the redemptive purposes of God in Jesus.[23] Others, however, suggest that Jesus is foretelling the destruction of the temple in Jerusalem after the Jewish leaders have attempted to silence him and his disciples.[24] The radical reversal of God's new realm will be announced, whether through voices that celebrate its reign or through the cries of those whose power is destroyed.

Throughout Luke's Gospel, "voice" is connected with the issues relating to authority, power, and truth. As the anointed prophet, Jesus' authority, power, and truth can be known by listening to his voice. His prophetic identity is also revealed when he silences oppressive forces and brings the oppressed to voice. This radical reversal is made possible through the boundless presence of the Holy Spirit with Jesus in ministry.

The disciples, however, remain remarkably silent throughout the story. Except for brief moments of recognition (e.g., Peter's confession in Luke 9), the disciples are mostly speechless. It is not until after his resurrection that Jesus commissions them to speak as witnesses of all that they have experienced and heard. Not until the disciples embrace the presence of the Holy Spirit themselves do they find their own voices.

Speaking of Pentecost

The drama of Luke-Acts takes an interesting turn following a brief intermission. A second event, much like the baptism of Jesus in Act One, defines the nature of the church's identity and ministry at the beginning of Act Two (the book of Acts). Through the outpouring of the Holy Spirit, the believers are commissioned and empowered for a prophetic ministry that models the ministry of Jesus. The result of the Spirit's presence with the disciples was the power to speak.

The Feast of Pentecost was one of three major festivals in the Jewish calendar. It originated as a harvest festival. After the exile, however, the character of Pentecost shifted toward the celebration of covenant renewal, with emphasis on God's covenants with Noah and Abraham.[25] The author of Luke-Acts may have naturally drawn connections between the event of Pentecost and the story of God's covenant with Israel through the encounter with Moses on Mount Sinai.

Have you ever experienced God through the human voice? "Yes," said Olivia. "Through the voice of a stranger." "Yes," said Alexis. "Through the voice of a professor. It was very unintentional on his part." "Yes," said Roz. "Through the voice of my grandmother."

The similarities between the establishment of the covenant at Mount Sinai and the giving of the Holy Spirit at Pentecost can be seen in the theological images employed in each narrative. The images of "fire" and "wind" are often associated with the human encounter of the "voice" of God. Rabbinic sources develop this idea, claiming that, as God spoke on the mountain, God's voice was so powerful that it became visible as fire. According to their tradition, the voice of God was divided into several voices or languages so that all people could understand the Law. At Pentecost, therefore, the divided tongues and wind could indicate that the voice of God was manifesting itself again to all the nations of the world, represented by the nationalities of pilgrims in Jerusalem. All humanity could understand the "new covenant" that was proclaimed through the voices of the disciples.[26]

Another image in the story seems strangely familiar. The events in Acts 2 are preceded by a scene in which Jesus disappears into a cloud, much the same way Moses did when he ascended the mountain to receive the Law. Of course, this same scene could allude to the departure of Elijah, resulting in the transfer of the prophetic Spirit to Elisha (2 Kings 2:9–14). In either case, the ascension could easily be related to the mystery of the Spirit's presence, connecting the Pentecost event with the prophetic tradition before it.

Equally compelling is the argument that the author of Luke-Acts is drawing connections between the Pentecost event and the baptism of Jesus.[27] The disciples, like Jesus before them, are engaged in prayer at the time of the outpouring of the Holy Spirit. The Spirit descends in a physical way, empowering them to speak. In this way, the baptism of the disciples at Pentecost equipped them to continue the prophetic ministry of Jesus before them.

Of particular importance in the story is the proclamation of the words taken from the prophet Joel. As a sign of the arrival of the new ordered realm of God, the Spirit is poured out on all people. The boundaries between race, gender, age, and status are erased, and the distinction between the public and private sphere is disregarded. The Spirit's presence makes possible a new community of equality and freedom. All kinds of ordinary people are empowered to speak.

The unfolding narrative of Luke-Acts is, therefore, an account of the transfer of the Spirit from the Messianic prophet to the community of faith. Much like the Old Testament story of Moses transferring the Spirit to the seventy elders (Numbers 11:25) the source of Jesus' prophetic ministry is offered to a community of people for the continuation of the prophetic task. Suddenly God's work is performed, not by the charismatic individual, but through a community of prophetic voices led by the Holy Spirit.

The evidence of this link is demonstrated in the disciples' ability to exercise the same prophetic powers as Jesus and the Old Testament prophets. The ability to discern hypocrisy and deception, the exercise of power over demons, the power to heal and comfort, and the capacity to unmask the unspoken thoughts of others were marks of the prophet.[28] The stories in Acts that follow the Pentecost event verify the disciples' endowment of remarkable gifts for their prophetic vocation.

The power of the Spirit to speak and proclaim the new ordered reality of God is given first to Jesus, the chosen of God. After his death and resurrection, the gift is transferred to the community of faith. The power to speak about a liberation that radically reverses the established order is distributed broadly to those who would follow in the prophetic pathway of Jesus. The purpose of speaking is identical: "to bring good news to the poor...to proclaim release to the captives and recovery of sight to the blind, to let the oppressed go free, to proclaim the year of the Lord's favor"(Luke 4:18–19). The truth of this proclamation is verified in the life, death, and resurrection of Jesus of Nazareth, who was anointed by the same Spirit.

Speaking of Stephen's Sermon

Nowhere in the book of Acts is the importance of "voice" more profoundly expressed than in the sermon of Stephen. The recovery of a personal, dynamic relationship with God through the Spirit is the subject of that sermon in Acts 7. Beginning with Abraham, the sermon recounts the establishment of the covenant. Abraham listened to God's voice and responded in faith. Likewise, Joseph responded to God's voice in faithfulness and, by the power of his own voice, saved his family in Egypt. Moses was given prophetic power. He defended the oppressed and exercised wisdom. He listened to the voice of God in the flame of a burning bush and found himself commissioned as liberator and judge. As leader of the exodus of the people Israel, he spoke directly to God at Mount Sinai and received "living oracles" to give to them.

The text goes on to explain that during the time of Moses, God ordered the creation of the tent of testimony, which could be carried with the people as the dwelling place for conversation with God. When Solomon built the temple as the house of God, the very nature of God was violated. God could not be contained in any material dwelling made by human hands. How could a building contain the voice of God!

The sermon ends with a scathing indictment of the religious establishment of the day. By accusing them of being "uncircumcised in heart and ears," the writer suggests that they are unprepared for a relationship that would involve listening to God's voice or expressing their own.[29] By opposing the Holy Spirit, they refused to allow the power of prophetic speech to have authority in their lives. They had substituted the law and the temple for the reality of God.

Stephen's sermon ends in violence as the people are moved to rage. They drag him out of the city and stone him to death. Stephen asks God to receive his spirit and to forgive those who rejected him (Acts 7:59-60). Once more, the announcement of the new order of God's realm, empowered by God's Spirit, provokes rejection of the prophet.

Speaking of Resistance

The evidence in Luke-Acts suggests that prophetic voices should expect rejection. The crowd's reaction to Stephen is but one example of an angry response to the prophetic speech of early Christians.

Peter and John were the first characters in Acts to experience resistance. On their way to the temple for prayer, they had spoken to a man in a way that resulted in a miraculous healing. The result gave Peter an opportunity to preach in the temple. This annoyed the religious leaders, and they had Peter and John arrested. When the two spoke boldly in defense of their actions, the leaders were surprised because the speakers were just ordinary people. When ordered not to speak or teach at all in the name of Jesus, Peter and John replied, "Whether it is right in God's sight to listen to you rather than to God, you must judge; for we cannot keep from speaking about what we have seen and heard" (Acts 4:19–20). Their authority for speaking came from hearing the voice of God through the power of the Holy Spirit.

Paul encountered a similar experience when working in Philippi (Acts 16). A slave girl was captive to an alien spirit, which made her follow Paul and cry out, "These men are slaves of the Most High God, who proclaim to you a way of salvation." Paul addressed the spirit and the girl was released from its power. [30] The owners of the slave were so angry about the loss of their investment that they rallied the crowd to demand that Paul and Silas be stripped, flogged, and thrown into jail.

After Paul made his way back to Jerusalem, he went to the temple. There his opponents tried to beat him to death but were stopped by soldiers. Paul was arrested; though imprisoned, he continued to speak to the chief priests and council, governors, and kings. His arrest ultimately led to his arrival in Rome, where he was held under house arrest for a number of years. [31] Paul's rejection by the Jewish leaders provided him the opportunity to speak to those with influence in the Roman Empire.

The theme of rejection is central to the unfolding plot of Luke-Acts. The final chapter of Acts ends with Paul's use of the words of the prophet Isaiah, "You will indeed listen, but never understand." God continues to speak, but religious leaders fail to recognize the presence of the Spirit because they are not expecting to hear the voice of God within a community of ordinary human voices. The covenant between God and humanity is still misunderstood.

Echoes

What an amazing story! The Holy Spirit, sacred *ruach,* breathes through women and men, old and young, single and married, slaves and free persons, Jew and non-Jew, and empowers them to speak with authority and truth. The same *ruach* disables the powerful, silences the demonic, and breathes life into death. The Spirit breathes through Jesus in a limitless way, combining into one single voice the harmony of the voices of prophets throughout the ages. In turn, Jesus promises power to the disciples, and the Spirit sweeps through their silence and draws forth multiple voices alive with the presence of God.

The power to call new worlds out of chaos can be extremely threatening to the voices that wish to name and control the world for their own benefit. Thus, the same story of the power and possibility through the Spirit is cluttered with bloody bodies that have endured imprisonment, mockery, beatings, stoning, and crucifixion. People continue to speak, however, because they hear the voice of God, they breathe the Spirit that cannot be contained, and they find that their voices offer a unique, unmistakable, essential tone to the sound of God's liberation of the world.

Can human speech reflect divine reality? Absolutely. The essence of God's agency demands it.

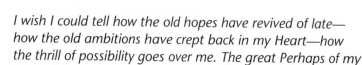

I wish I could tell how the old hopes have revived of late—how the old ambitions have crept back in my Heart—how the thrill of possibility goes over me. The great Perhaps of my Future haunts me & makes me full of hope. God has given me more power than I have used.

Frances E. Willard[1]

I believe we do more for those in our care by teaching them about the silence of God than we do by trying to explain it away. By addressing the experience of God's silence in scripture and in our listeners' own lives, we may be able to open up the possibility that silence is as much a sign of God's presence as of God's absence—that divine silence is not a vacuum to be filled but a mystery to be entered into, un-armed with words and distracted by noise—a holy of holies in which we too may be struck dumb by the power of the unsayable God. Our job is not to pierce that mystery with language but to reverence it.

Barbara Brown Taylor[2]

We do not preach for any reason except that God has called us and seeks to use our voices for the liberation of humanity. So when we preach God's redemptive word, guess what? Our voices, our piping, little sin-struck, frightened, underpaid, hesitant voices just happen to be the voice of God. Imagine that—please, oh please, imagine that!

David G. Buttrick[3]

Chapter 4

Commitment to Conversation: An Emerging Theology of Voice

In the beginning, God spoke. The recorded witness of the Jewish-Christian tradition begins with the sound of God speaking the world into being. The Spirit, *ruach* or breath, moved at creation to bring forth life. The Spirit that called forth creation first flowed through the being of God, animating it with sound, so that the being of God stood in sharp relief to the chaos of the surrounding universe. The agency that plainly brought the reality of creation into contrast with chaos, giving it value and integrity, was the same agency that allowed creation to know the reality of the divine. The sound of the voice, therefore, is the location of spiritual creativity—the evidence of divine life.

To be made in the image of God is to be made in the sound of God. In the beginning, only the sound of the Creator gives evidence of God's being. There is no "image" available to sight. When the Spirit, *ruach* or breath of life, flowed through the human creature, it gave the Human One the agency to announce her own existence and name reality with the sound of voice.

The sound of voice, then, gave the creator and creation integrity, value and agency.

Beyond that, the voice made it possible for God and the Human One to express a relationship of mutuality that provided an intimate and on-going connection. Voice is about recognizing and valuing the existence of the other, calling forth the other into a response of conversation, and claiming the priority of mutuality over the static separation of silence.

That is why, over and over, the Biblical witness records the conversation between God and humankind as a calling out to one another.

Covenant, exchanged between the voices of God and humanity, is an ongoing relationship of hearing and speaking in the present moment. Covenant, at its foundation, is about presence with the other through voice. Through speaking, God allows Godself to be known in sharp relief to the cloudy unknown of the universe. Through listening to God's voice, human beings know the person of God in the present moment, making possible the binding commitment to ongoing relationship. By creating human beings with the same ability to speak, God commits Godself to listening to that voice and continuing to respond—an act of love and care. Therefore, the sustaining of the conversation into the present moment is the essence of covenant, for speaking and listening are the evidence of the continuing life of the creator and creation.

The purpose of religious life is to assist and sustain the conversation between God and humanity. Whenever people fail to hear the voice of God, God continues to call. God, unwilling to remain silent or removed from relationship to humanity, restores community time and time again. Religious speech flourishes within this dynamic.

By creating all living beings in the "sound" of God, God gave each individual the power to announce her or his existence, to be known. In return, each person has the ability to recognize the voice of the other, to claim the value of the voices of other people by knowing and responding. The reality of God's relationship with humanity, the source of life through creation, is extended between human beings, as well.

Of course, this model remains ideal only as a three-way conversation (God to humanity, person to person, and humanity to God) continues to flow out of mutual recognition and love. As soon as voices begin to compete for ascendancy and dominion over other voices, the conversation breaks down. In a triadic arrangement, the flow of conversation requires equal acknowledgement of the value of the other voices while continuing to claim the value of the self in relation. As soon as one party stops listening to another, the relationship is broken.

Into this brokenness, God's *ruach* or breath animates the voice of prophets to call people back into relationship. The prophet is first a listener, attuned to the voice of God as a way of knowing. The prophet also listens to the voice of the people, a way of loving those made in the image of God. In addition, the prophet is aware of the sound of her own voice as the source of divine power and life. The urgency of relationship comes through this integrated "knowing" of the prophet in a given context, making it impossible for the prophet "not to speak." The desire for the restoration of covenant conversation, the essence of life itself, compels the prophet to speak. Initiated by God, the voice of the prophet is a force that cannot be contained by silence.

When the dynamic, triangular relationship between God, humanity, and self is restored, the voice becomes the locus of life-giving creativity in the world once more. God continues the process of calling new worlds into being through the sound of voice. The "new order of God" or the "realm of God" is about the full and equal valuing of self, world, and God in an ongoing, contemporary way. The only way that we can experience the full essence of this realm is through voice—by claiming our own value and power as a real gift of divine wisdom and by listening to the voice of God and others as the continuing source of life and love.

This life-giving creativity was expressed most fully in Jesus, the one who came preaching about the new ordered realm of God. Jesus' authority for prophetic vocation came from the same Spirit that breathed life into creation in the beginning. His authority was expressed through voice. The integrity of his life lay in the congruity between his actions and speech in relation to God's action and speech.

Resistance to Jesus' ministry came from voices that refused to allow free and mutual conversation among human beings and with God. The demonic voices that choked out the true voices of individual persons feared Jesus' ability to dissolve their power over others. Political and religious voices sought to silence Jesus when he challenged the hierarchies of power that gave some human voices preeminence over others, silencing massive groups of people for the benefit of a few. Deceptive voices challenged Jesus, from the beginning of his ministry, to exercise the power that was inherent in his voice to exploit the earth, human beings, and God to his own advantage, a temptation that was rejected by Jesus.

The effort to silence Jesus by putting him to death failed. Into the emerging chaos of misplaced authority, God spoke, bringing life from the silence of death. Following his resurrection, Jesus came and stood among his followers and "breathed on them" (John 20:22). They, like Jesus, were given power to be the agents of creation, prophetic voices made in the sound of God.

The prophetic authority of Jesus' voice was transferred to the voices of all who sought the realm of God. Communities of people, not just lone prophets, were empowered by the Spirit to listen to God, others, and self in a way that compelled them to speak. The community sought to live out of a dynamic relationship that sustained the mutual conversation among human beings and God. The voice of the community of faith became embodied in individual voices addressing particular situations and contexts. The life-giving creativity of the community's voice met resistance as it challenged the established order. The voice could not be silenced, however, because it derived its authority from the ongoing divine conversation.

This power to speak is ours today through the same Spirit, *ruach* or breath, that moved through God at creation, compelled prophets to speak, authorized the vocation of Jesus, and animated a new community of amazing symphonic character. We must claim that power for ourselves and others in relation to the sound of God's voice. To remain silent is to fail to acknowledge our value as human beings made in the "sound" of God. To remain silent is to prevent ourselves from being "known" and, therefore, being part of the life-giving conversation with others. To remain silent is to deny the continuing creativity of God to draw "new worlds" into the present and future moments.

To claim our own voice as a reflection of the divine in us, then, demands that we also learn to listen. If our voice is valuable and powerful, so is the voice of God that brought it into being; so is the distinctive voice that is possible in each unique individual. We must speak while hearing each other into speech. This is the way of salvation.

Our Protestant Heritage

God's voice. Human voice. The relationship between them raises an important and challenging set of questions for preaching. Those who have pondered these complex questions throughout the centuries have found various answers. No answer has been completely satisfying, for answers are always partial, leading to greater paradox and ambiguity. Perhaps a complete understanding will always remain a little outside our grasp. What is preaching? Who is the preacher? These basic questions, if asked honestly and openly, have the potential to lead us continually to new terrain, new understandings, perhaps liberating ones.

We are the inheritors of a great Protestant tradition of the Word. The Word historically has been the central focus of worship as communities have gathered together for nurture, healing, guidance, and sustenance. That inheritance, forged by the reformers in a climate of resistance, and sealed in this century by neoorthodox thinking, lays before us an understanding of Word sent from a wholly transcendent God, and spoken through biblical texts.

We could not capture the complexity of thought in the Reformers, or in Karl Barth of our own century, in single or simple statements. To pull quotes about preaching out of their contexts would caricature their contributions and do violence to them, as surely as ripping one biblical verse out of its context can alter or diminish its meaning. Yet, it could be said that inherent in the thought of these is an understanding of the preacher as spokesperson, mediator, mouthpiece, or vessel. Sermon, then, is the occasion for hearing "a voice beyond the preacher's voice, the very word of the living God."[4] While Barth, for instance, has an understanding of the preacher as one who can be challenged, contradicted, or "loosened up" by what is read in the biblical text, the preacher "himself" does not hold the gospel in "his" own heart or thought. Rather,

> It is not the function of the preacher to reveal God or to act as his intermediary when the gospel is preached. God speaks; there is no question of the preacher revealing anything or of a revelation being conveyed through him. Revelation is a closed system in which God is the subject, the object, the middle term.[5]

This idea is not unlike those of Protestant theologian John Calvin, who speaks about the community of "man" used by God to declare God's will to us by mouth. This, he indicates, is a delegated work. Through mouths God "may do his own work, just as a workman uses a tool."[6] Neither is it unlike the ideas of Martin Luther, who said in a sermon on the Easter Gospel,

> So, the pastor must be sure that God speaks through his mouth. Otherwise it is time for him to be quiet. Yes, I hear the sermon, but who is speaking? The minister? No, indeed! You do not hear the minister. True the voice is his, but my God is speaking the word which he preaches or speaks.[7]

For Barth, the Bible is the Word of God or becomes the Word of God as it is being preached to the community. The preacher, he warned, must have absolute confidence in scripture so that preaching is exposition of it. A preacher is not concerned with self; rather, the preacher is caught up in the text and "his" regard for it so that there is room for nothing else. The sermon is like an "involuntary lip movement" of one who reads with care, attention, and surprise so that the community will know that the preacher has not written the text from which the sermon is preached. The preacher is modest, under the constant scrutiny of the text. The preacher must step back with any personal views on spirituality. The gospel is not in the preacher's thoughts or heart. It is in scripture.[8] A "theology of voice" that takes seriously the voice of the preacher challenges this notion of an unchanging and static Word that somehow comes to expression through women and men unaltered and unscathed.

A New Look

Calling upon the thoughts and insights of those who have helped us think about the importance and value of language within community, Fred Craddock more recently turned our attention from "word" to "spoken word" in *As One Without Authority.*[9] His intention in writing this volume was clearly to challenge old ways of forming the sermon and to offer a new alternative. His discussion of inductive movement, however, is preceded by careful attention to voice; this attention serves as an unsuspecting prelude to the issues at hand.

Craddock leads us into the world of the "spoken word" by describing for us its character and value. He discusses written word; it is restrictive. It limits communication to transcendent statements of information. Spoken word, on the other hand, effects participation and communication. All meaning is not provided by the speaker; much has to do with the listener. The spoken word is dialogical. It is spontaneous. Spoken words are not past. Neither are they future. They are of the present. There is in spoken word the potential for change, uncertainty, openness to interruption, insecurity. This lack of finality opens to the interior life. Speaking is direct, personal, engaging, demanding, precarious, and vulnerable. Craddock goes on to reflect on the "sermon moment," and about fashioning oral proclamation to allow space for the listener to participate in the sermon's telling and experience.[10]

Even through Craddock's remarks about the "spoken word" (or voice) are brief, they serve as a welcome invitation to readers to think about a theology of voice for preaching. By concentrating on "voice" as the locus of God's agency and being, this theology of preaching shifts its emphasis from the more rigid and singular Word of God (as evidenced in the Refomers and in Barth) to an event of dialogue between the text and diverse voices that know of different life contexts, understandings, and experiences. In this understanding of preaching, then, the canon becomes no longer a slate of norms, but offers "models of struggles and emerging visions" that, through the leading of God's spirit, open us up to potential transformations. The notion of a Word from God that freezes revelation at a particular point in time and within a particular text promotes disempowerment. Persons no longer take responsibility for participating in meaning-making. They are passive recipients of truth.

The movement from an understanding of "word" to "voice" opens up the possibility for dialogue and renewal. "Word" implies less a God who speaks than one who has spoken. A metaphor of "voice" suggests that the Holy Spirit still speaks, gives voice to ongoing revelation in the lives of many who have been silenced, often in the name of the very God who is thus represented. A theology of a static and unchanging "Word" cannot incorporate the voices of God that echo in the lives of diverse beings created in God's sound.[11]

A theology of voice for preaching, then, suggests that the preacher must listen carefully to the text and, *also*, to revelations that come to her through her experience in the world. The word is contextualized through her understanding and those of her community. The speaking/listening God continues to be present, bringing new insight, challenging a fraudulent finality of understanding. The preacher, then, is no mere mouthpiece, herald, or vessel of the word. The preacher is in covenant with the one who has created her and given her a distinctive voice. The preacher is called to bring what she has, all that she has, to the task of preaching, immersing herself imaginatively in it, naming the world, and listening for the new thing that is ever being created. Such preaching requires thought, emotion, and imagination.

Richard Thulin has articulated questions raised in response to such an understanding of revelatory experience.[12] If, for instance, one's experience runs counter to the church's traditional interpretation of the Bible, on which authority does one depend? There is the danger of universalizing an experience that is very particular. If one asserts that one's experience need not be tested or that it does not need validation from outside persons, then it may violate the interpretation of reality within community. Or,

> I was reading *Conversations with God, Uncommon Dialogue*. In it, the author asks if word or experience is ultimate to us. Words express experience only. The experience is the ultimate. Does that make our experience revelation? Yes! We put so much emphasis on the Word, that when our experience contradicts the Word we don't want to believe in it. But how can you not believe in your experience? It is yours!
>
> *CW*

> The Holy Spirit is about experience. It is about lived experience.
>
> *COD*

more dangerous, one may use one's own experience to test and validate all other experiences. There is also, he says, the danger of fabrication, the danger that what is recited is fictionalized, half-remembered, over-sentimentalized, and more than favorably interpreted for the occasion. There is the danger of self-deception. These and other dangers are real. Yet, these dangers are diminished and offset by an understanding of the prophetic preacher not only as one who speaks out of life experience but also as one who listens with a prophetic ear. This is the preacher open to hearing the challenging, confronting word of the text, of God, of community, of others whose life experiences speak differently.

Yes, there are dangers, but are they not risks worth taking? What is the alternative? What are the dangers of believing in a static word, a God who does not speak but has spoken, a God divorced from our own living, breathing experiences in life as we live it?

Any understanding that undermines and contradicts the belief in the incarnation of the "Word" becomes divorced from life. *A theology of the "Word" apart from a theology of "Voice" is contrary to our understanding of the gospel.* The "Word" can become wedded in our minds to singular interpretations that have been born out of one climate, worldview, or personal perspective. The Word of God is more multi-dimensional, complex, dynamic than that; the Word is open to question and criticism and revision. We have learned that from reading the biblical text itself. It needs different ears to listen to it, different voices to express it, different voices to liberate it from its heavy, restrictive, patriarchal, choking action. Word of God is always an interpreted word.

In 1888, Frances Willard published a volume entitled *Woman in the Pulpit.* She was an advocate for women, insisting that the "stereoscopic" view of truth evident in the biblical text could be heard only when men and women together discerned the perspective of the Bible's full-orbed revelation. Hers was one of the early voices crying on the frontier for an egalitarian pulpit, believing that an understanding of the gospel demanded it.[13]

Said yet another way, the gospel cries out for contextualization. That is the gospel's own hermeneutic. This perspective on the importance of the life experience of the preacher and her need to bring that experience to preaching is beginning to be evidenced in small and, at first glance, insignificant ways. Contemporary homileticians are calling for preachers to be attentive to, and to give voice to, their own distinctive ways of bringing a word to the gathered community. Richard Ward, for instance, in *Speaking from the Heart* discusses the congruity between "one's voice and presence for speaking and the deep and inner voices that arise in our private and communal selves."[14] Thomas Troeger, in *The Parable of Ten Preachers*, tells us the story of a fictive homiletics professor named Peter Linden who teaches a class entitled "Preachers in Search of Their Voices." The professor had an understanding of the preacher's self that convinced him that every preacher had a "voice"—a distinctive pattern of substance and expression that could be traced from sermon to sermon.[15] In *The Embodied Word*, Charles Rice also identifies the voice with the preacher herself. "This voice, the preacher, speaks among and for a community that has been saying these words and living with these symbols for a long time, but freshly, so as to 'try them out' in the face of what is happening in the here and now."[16] Rice recalls the words of Joseph Sittler, who speaks of the recognizable human voice—an instrument more subtle and versatile than any instrument in an orchestra. The voice has the possibility of re-calling the past, meeting the present, and suggesting the future. The word of God comes to us embodied in person.[17]

Christine Smith has provided the homi-letic world with one of the first extensive treat-ments of feminism and preaching in *Weaving the Sermon*. In this volume, the rich and multi-faceted dimensions of voice come into play. She acknowledges one of the most difficult dimen-sions related to women and preaching: learn-ing to trust that voice.[18]

> Women's experience is often consciously censored; thus, the words of the female preacher sometimes become "frozen." A learning must take place. The female preacher must come to understand that she has the right and the ability to be there.
>
> *ASU*

Even these brief excerpts from contem-porary homiletical literature suggest the im-portance of the preacher's self and voice in the sermon event. They hint of an immanent God who speaks and of a Spirit who inspires and enters our human experience. They hint of a Word that is dynamic and changing and eager to meet and challenge our contexts and to be in conversation with them. These excerpts imply that the preacher is called to model God, by continuously bringing her heart and mind to the task, because what she thinks and feels is important and revelatory. In these understandings the preacher with her speech is ca-pable of drawing new worlds out of the old in her own distinctive, au-thentic, authoritative way.

What does this theology of preaching look like when the preacher is called to bring a word in a climate of resistance? When she is marginalized from the pulpit? On what can this woman depend? "Because of consistent opposition to their exercise of public ministry, from both genders, women who would preach have been forced to rely upon sources of authority other than ecclesiastical, and sources of support other than hierarchical."[19] Thus, women do not hold tightly to external authorities. There are forces, strong and pervasive, at work in the world that try to silence them. They can only trust the One who has called them, inspired them, and blessed them.

Women know all too well the silenced nature of women's experience and women's stories, and are becoming increasingly committed to giving a voice and an honored place to those who have gone before us.

Christine Smith[1]

Even as a strategy for promoting feminism, separation neglects the need to transform the order not only for ourselves, but for others: for the dead and those who have suffered, the living who do not yet speak, and those not yet born who will have voices to speak.

Rebecca Chopp[2]

Chapter 5

Context and Voice: Stories from History

Women finding voice for preaching is not a new phenomenon brought on by the second phase of American feminism in the 1970's. Throughout history, women have been speaking of and from their experience of divine reality. However, the historical context has not always allowed women's voices to be heard in the public arena, nor has it preserved the content of women's speech for generations to come. For centuries, the recorders and preservers of religious history have been men. Therefore, anyone's speech, if preserved, had to be filtered through the dominant perspective held by males. Women's speech has often resided on dusty shelves in obscure libraries, or it has been lost completely.

Fortunately for women today, the scholarship spawned by the feminist critique of the 1970's and 1980's has highlighted the limitations of masculine interpretations of reality. At the same time, it has recovered valuable voices that offer echoes of women's perspectives throughout history. The "hermeneutic of suspicion" has reintroduced women to the sound of their own silence through the ages, while encouraging stifled voices to speak anew in today's culture.

Telling their stories has always been a way for women to authorize their own reality. As we listen to each other's stories, we begin to make sense of our own. We have chosen four stories of women to illustrate the process of women finding voice in different contexts. Each context offers us a different look at how women's voices are discovered, how they are silenced (whether consciously or not), how these voices are expressed, and how women find an audience in spite of the layers of opposition that seek to silence them.

The Story of Mary Magdalene, Joanna, Mary the Mother of James, and the Other Women at the Resurrection

At the end of Luke's Gospel, the event of Jesus' resurrection is introduced by the story of the women at the tomb, a basic story shared by all the Synoptic Gospels. Luke's version differs from the others, however, in a way that highlights the ironic tension within the story of the women's testimony to the resurrection. The credibility and power of the church's earliest proclamation that "Jesus is risen" seemed to be negatively altered in some way when pronounced by the lips of women.

The story actually begins with the women standing before the cross, witnessing the cruel death of Jesus from a distance. In loyalty, the women remain at the site as Jesus' body is dislodged from the cross. They accompany the body to the tomb. None of them could ever be uncertain that Jesus had not truly died, or had not actually been buried.

When Jesus came announcing a new order several months before, these women had found a new identity in the "family" or "household" of Jesus' followers (Luke 8:21). They provided financial support and service for the members of this new community of faith. They listened and learned the tradition of the new family. This new household of Jesus transcended many barriers created by the established family system of that day, reordering social relationships. Just as if Jesus were a brother, the followers of Jesus assumed responsibility at his death for proper preparation of the body for burial. Fully intending to anoint the body for burial as soon as the Sabbath had passed, these same women quickly gathered spices and ointments for that task before abandoning their work in obedience to the law.[3]

The faithfulness of the women in fulfilling their responsibilities to Jesus provided an opportunity for them to be the first to encounter the reality of the resurrection. At the close of the Sabbath, the women resumed the duties that they had temporarily delayed. Carrying with them the necessary embalming spices, they found the stone rolled away from the tomb. Stepping into the encircling darkness, they found nothing but emptiness. Jesus' body was not there.

These close friends struggled to make sense of this surprising turn of events. As if in response to their flood of questions, two unexpected persons, dressed in dazzling apparel, appeared and spoke to them.[4] In spite of the cultural taboos against speaking to women in private, the two men addressed the women, guiding them to understand what they were experiencing. The two treated the women as informed disciples, not as mere messengers whose primary purpose was to transfer words to the men.

The words of the two strangers were directed to them: "Remember how he told you, while he was still in Galilee, that the Human One must be handed over to sinners, and be crucified, and on the third day rise again." In response, the women *remembered* what Jesus had said. In order to "remember," the women had to have known Jesus' teaching. They had listened, retained, and understood his words. Like their friends Mary and Martha (Luke 10:38–42), these women were considered trustworthy and faithful followers of Jesus.

The women's response to the two at the tomb stands in sharp contrast to the disciples' response on the mountain of transfiguration. In the story of the transfiguration (Luke 9:28–36), the three disciples drew the wrong conclusions about the significance of the two men conversing with Jesus, and they ended up keeping silent about what they had witnessed. In contrast, the women at the tomb not only understood the message of the two figures but also acted upon their knowledge by telling others about the revelation.

This is different from the other gospel stories in which the women were commissioned to "go and tell" the others about what they had seen and heard. As if the "truth" of the resurrection event could not be contained in the experiences of a few women at the tomb, the other gospels imply that the "truth" arose from the authority of the two men who gave the women the message to convey. In Luke's account, however, the women returned from the tomb and told the other disciples what had transpired, not because they were commissioned, but because they themselves were informed disciples who understood the significance of their experience. In other words, Luke, the author of this resurrection story, wished to affirm the credibility of the women's experience.[5]

> The women's service leads them to a tomb which they find to be empty, to a body that is no longer there—among the dead. In this situation, the women are reaffirmed as hearers of the word: they are the first to hear the message of the resurrection proclaimed, and this calls to their remembrance the word they once heard from Jesus. This makes them leave the tomb behind, and they go forth and tell everything to the eleven and to all the others. As has been mentioned earlier, no commission is given to the women in Luke's version of the story. Their witness is due to their own spontaneous initiative as a continuation of what they themselves have heard and remembered. The women appear as the first witnesses of the Lord Jesus' resurrection, and the narrative in

Luke 24 says nothing about any hesitation or confusion or fear on their part as they make their way from the grave—unlike the narratives in Mark and Matthew. The narrative itself guarantees for the reader that the women are trustworthy and credible witnesses and speak the truth.[6]

The evidence of the truthfulness of the women's claim is established in the language and structure of the story itself. Suddenly the reader is brought face-to-face with specific women, named and identified (24:10). In doing so, the author provides evidence that adds to the credibility of the women's story. To reinforce the truth of their claim even more, the story of these women is recalled by the male disciples in the Emmaus story (Luke 24:22–24). With all of this evidence, the women should have been believed.

In the story, however, the disciples did not believe. The women's words "seemed to them an idle tale." After all, the Jewish culture of that time would not accept as credible the witness of a lone woman without a male witness to corroborate the testimony. So instead of trusting the word of the women, Peter leaped up and visited the tomb himself, thereby providing a credible (male) witness to the same event. He returned with the same story. Thus, the women could be believed after all.

The many women of Luke's gospel were participants in birthing the new order of God through bearing Jesus into the world, prophesying about his future, providing financial backing for his ministry, hosting and hearing Jesus as teacher and friend, following as disciples, and staying with him through death. These women had a direct relationship with the one they believed in. Although these women were the primary and credible recipients of the truth, they could not be believed because they were suspect in the eyes of the broader culture. Therefore, the author could not present them as the sole authorities for such an important claim as the resurrection of Jesus.[7]

At the end of the story, the women's inherent power and full partnership is sacrificed by male authorship, making the message palatable to a culture that was unwilling to accept women as full and equal partners in religious community. The author of Luke seemed to create the literary necessity of a corroborating male witness in this story to make it agreeable to the broader culture. Ironically, the clear and credible voices of Mary Magdalene, Joanna, Mary the mother of James, and the others were dismissed and silenced in favor of masculine spokespersons who were not direct witnesses, but had access to the public trust.

This story, along with others, reveals a certain irony in the message of Luke-Acts. It reflects how the particular social context that was structured by strict gender boundaries affected the retelling of the story itself. An examination of Luke's writing reveals that it contains more references to women than the other Synoptic Gospels. Not only are women mentioned and named more often in Luke's Gospel, but they are also portrayed as exercising an active role in the community of Jesus' followers. It is interesting to discover, however, that the appearance and responsibility of women diminishes significantly as the narrative unfolds throughout the book of Acts. The author portrays women as having withdrawn to a more subordinate role in the Christian movement, an attitude that is in keeping with the cultural model inherited from Jewish tradition. It is not, however, reflective of the actions and attitudes of Jesus toward women.

In her well-documented study of the role of women in Luke-Acts, Turid Karlsen Seim argues that this particular story highlights the authority of women's speech at the same time that it acknowledges the influences of culture that are at work to discredit them. Elisabeth Schüssler Fiorenza and others would argue that the construction of Luke-Acts has contributed to the process of making women invisible in the church.[8] The tension within the text suggests that outside cultural norms exerted an unrelenting pressure on the early church as it developed its new identity as a community of faith.

If women were permitted to tell their own story, perhaps this narrative would have ended much differently. Unfortunately, the many accounts of women's experience have not been preserved and validated by the church. Any attempts by women to author their own account of the "Christ event" were crushed by the early church as it developed respectability within the dominant culture. The desire of church leaders to satisfy the powerful patrons of the movement led to their insistence upon uniformity of doctrine, a move that would stifle many dissenting voices, including the voices of women. In order to preserve the integrity of their own experience, women must learn to recount and interpret their own stories for the sake of the larger community.

Nevertheless, Luke's story of the women at the tomb bears an interesting irony for today's church. This very text that signaled the move of the early church to modify its message for the approval of popular culture is a text to which contemporary women have turned as an authority for their own experience of being called by God to preach. Efforts to silence the voices of the women have failed. The clear and credible voices of

Mary Magdalene, Joanna, Mary the mother of James, and the others continue to linger as a distinguishable counterpoint to the intended melody of the text. Although the text continues to present women's testimony in a questionable light, the persistent credibility of the women's own witness makes real the event of resurrection for many hearers today.

The Story of Hildegard of Bingen

The Old and New Testament canon preserved stories and sayings about women that were recorded by a community captive to patriarchy. In this way, the accounts often reflect the values of the culture out of which the literature arose. As a result, those cultural assumptions about women embedded in the Bible continued to exert influences on Christian theology long after the cultural contexts had evolved.

During the medieval period, Christian attitudes about women were drawn from Jewish tradition as it had been influenced by Greek thought. The Jewish tradition had long emphasized the submission of women and their withdrawal from public life, a view that is echoed in the Pauline epistles. Greek writers described women as defective males, vessels for a process of human reproduction that originated with men.[9] These traditions often inferred that all women were unclean, or lacking wholeness.

The male theologians within the early church made their own contributions to negative attitudes toward women by their emphasis on Eve's sin, which introduced evil into the world. Eve was used as a prototype for all females, and women were demonized as wicked temptresses who were out to corrupt all humanity. Tertullian charged all women with responsibility for the depravity in the world, claiming that because of women "even the Son of God had to die." Saint Clement echoed the scathing indictment by exhorting women to be overwhelmed with shame at being a woman. Being born female was considered a curse that brought disgrace and abasement to all women.[10]

The medieval writers in Europe perpetuated this misogynist perspective by often stereotyping all women as willful and deceptive. One German writer painted Eve as daring to do what was forbidden her and wanting whatever would cause dishonor. Then, in a blanket statement, he declared all women "daughters of Eve." Conversely, he claimed the women who acted virtuously were, in spirit, really men. A Frenchman of the same era defended the right of husbands to physically abuse their wives because of their inherent sinfulness and need of correction.[11] How could the women who lived within this medieval worldview ever imagine living beyond the "curse" of their own "inherently evil natures"!

Amazingly, some women did. In spite of indictments against their gender, women arose to speak powerfully and prophetically during this period. Early in life, these women found their own voices and were compelled to exercise them for the sake of themselves and others.

- Clare of Assisi (1195–1253), influenced by the preaching of Francis, withdrew from traditional expectations, evaded her family, served the poor, established an order of women, and wrote her own rule for monastic life.
- Mechthild of Magdeburg (1210?–1297?) lived among the Beguines for a period of time before taking up residence with the Benedictine Order at Helfta. In this environment, she blossomed as a writer whose expositions on the direct union of the human being with the divine gave new definition to the intensity and power of holy love.
- Catherine of Siena (1347–1380) was a visionary and Dominican sister whose spiritual journey began with feeding her own household and enlarged to embrace the political and cultural needs of the larger society. In the end she wrote the *Dialogue* as an expression of the rich spiritual experience that was her life.
- Julian of Norwich (1342–1416?) enclosed herself as an anchoress of the parish church of Saint Julian in Conisford at Norwich. From there she advised many spiritual pilgrims and recorded in writing her encounters with God.[12]

Before the emergence of these women mystics, however, there was Hildegard of Bingen (1098–1179). As the tenth child born to a noble family, Hildegard was dedicated by her parents to God, perhaps as an act of "tithing" or because they were running low on dowry. In any case, when she was only eight years old, Hildegard was entrusted to the care of Jutta von Sponheim, who became a leader of the female community attached to the monastery of Disibodenberg. Under her tutelage, Hildegard studied theology, literature, and philosophy and learned to write in both German and Latin.[13]

In 1136 Hildegard was elected abbess of the community after Jutta's death. As leader, she made the controversial decision to leave the monastery in Disibodenberg, take the sisters and their dowries, and move to a new cloister in Rupertsberg near the town of Bingen. This decision was precipitated by the growth of the community due to her increasing fame as a preacher and writer, and her resistance to practices of the monastic community and the local authorities to which she was subject. In spite of the abbot's rejection of her request, she persisted in her appeals until the abbot finally granted her permission to leave.

Conflicts with the male clergy did not end with her move to Rupertsberg, however. She continued to intervene in the schismatic situation created in part by the Emperor Frederick Barbarossa. Even near the end of her life, Hildegard was the center of controversy for permitting the burial of a nobleman who had been excommunicated, but who was reconciled to the church during his last hours. Her actions resulted in an interdict against her and her convent that prevented them from celebrating the mass or singing the divine office. Eventually, in true Hildegardian form, she won her case and the interdict was lifted.

Besides her active and forceful leadership within her order, Hildegard was known for her writings. In addition to letters and music, her writing includes a trilogy of major works that describe her visions and interpret them. *Scivias* or *Know the Ways* (of the Lord), was her first book composed between 1141 and 1158; *Liber vitae meritorum* or *The Book of the Merits of Life* was written between 1158-1163; and *Liber divinorum operum* or *The Book of Divine Works* was completed in 1173.[14]

In the preface to the *Scivias*, Hildegard tells her own story of the experience of a prophetic call that gave her the power to speak about her knowledge of God. She began writing the *Scivias* when she was forty-two years old. Since the age of five, she had experienced "visions" which took the form of a brilliant light. As a child, she kept these visions to herself, unsure of their origin or meaning. Later in life, however, she experienced the voice of God commanding her to write. The light gave her an "infused knowledge" of scripture and the ability to interpret her visions.

In the story of her prophetic call, Hildegard admits to the struggle to express her own voice. Her story begins with a voice from Heaven speaking to her,

> O fragile human, ashes of ashes, and filth of filth! Say and write what you see and hear. But since you are timid in speaking, and simple in expounding, and untaught in writing, speak and write these things not by the requirements of human composition, but as you see and hear them on high in the heavenly places in the wonders of God. Explain these things in such a way that the hearer, receiving the words of his instructor, may expound them

in those words, according to that will, vision and instruction. Thus, therefore, O human, speak these things that you see and hear. And write them not by yourself or any other human being, but by the will of Him Who knows, sees and disposes all things in the secrets of His mysteries.

The voice repeated a second time:

Speak therefore of these wonders, and, being so taught, write them and speak.[15]

Within the convent, Hildegard had authority as the spiritual head of the household. In the outside world, for which she wrote, a woman's voice could hold no authority unless it could attribute its knowledge and wisdom to an external source. During the Middle Ages, prophecy was usually considered the uttering of divine secrets, a privileged knowledge reserved for those who were specially gifted to receive such revelation. Humility and weakness were characteristics of persons specifically chosen by God to "confound the strong." These were considered feminine attributes in that day. Perhaps for these reasons, Hildegard readily experienced the dissolution of her individual voice in order to acquire the authoritative voice for prophetic speech. The denial of her own voice and her self-identification as a mystical prophet allowed her to be taken seriously by others outside the convent.

Descriptions of her visioning give dramatic emphasis to the intensity of the physical and emotional impact of the experience:

It happened…when I was forty-two years and seven months old, Heaven was opened and a fiery light of exceeding brilliance came and permeated my whole brain, and inflamed my whole heart and my whole breast, not like a burning but like a warming flame, as the sun warms anything its rays touch. And immediately I knew the meaning of the exposition of the Scriptures…But I had sensed in myself wonderfully the power and mystery of secret and admirable visions from my childhood—that is, from the age of five— up to that time…This, however, I showed to no one except a few religious persons who were living in the same manner as I;…I concealed it in quiet silence. But the visions I saw I did not perceive in dreams, or sleep, or delirium, or by the eyes of the body, or by the ears of the outer self, or in hidden places; but I received them while awake and seeing with a pure mind and the eyes and ears of the inner self, in open places, as God willed it. How this might be is hard for mortal flesh to understand.[16]

Contemporary scholars have suggested that her visions may have actually been the symptoms of "scintillating scotoma," a form of migraine headache.[17] After experiencing these episodes for forty years, she learned to interpret these experiences as a gift from God. Coming to view her peculiar traits as somehow valuable and acceptable may have been an important step in her journey toward public voice.

Hildegard describes the moment she received her prophetic call as a transition into maturity in which she "passed out of childhood." Her process of resistance had led her into a psychosomatic illness that eventually confined her to a sickbed. Her distress and pain were attributed to the work of the Holy Spirit in taking away her security and pride; she was overwhelmed with guilt so that she would have no sense of personal gain from her prophetic role.

Her illness subsided, however, when she located someone to help her begin writing. Her close friend, Richardis of Stade, recruited Volmar of Disibodenberg, who became her faithful scribe, sharing in her work on *Scivias* for ten years. Perhaps the presence of a male counterpart made her feel more self-confident about the enterprise.

Her personal story ends, as it begins, with the external voice from Heaven commanding her to "cry out therefore, and write thus!" Such a command gives the reader a sense of the compelling urgency with which she expressed the spiritual message contained in her writings.[18]

For a long time she resisted going public with her abnormal experiences. It took the support and encouragement of male authorities for her finally to express her voice. Troubled by this compelling command to speak, she sought the advice of Saint Bernard who encouraged her to proceed. She dictated her words to a scribe, Volmar, who stayed with her throughout most of her life. When the work was partially completed, the abbot of Disibodenberg sent a copy to the archbishop of Mainz, who, in turn, presented it to Pope Eugenius. At the Synod of Trier, Pope Eugenius read it to the assembly and gave his approval to her writing. As a result, her works were met with widespread acceptance, which led to her popularity as a preacher and as a consultant to civic and church leaders alike.

Hildegard's *Scivias*, though filled with unusual images and meanings, was accepted by the powerful elite of the church because it reflected a sensitivity to the theological movement inspired by Saint Anselm in the previous century. Anselm had introduced a dimension of "inner growth" that extended beyond the traditional ideas of humility and obedience as disciplines leading to union with God. His emphasis on an intense, personal relationship with God promoted the work of individual meditation and visioning as avenues to a direct experience of the divine. As this spiritual theology flourished, a growing confidence in the individual and an emphasis on the unlimited love of God led to a celebration of individual ecstatic experience as the evidence of true piety.[19] Hildegard's visions reflect a direct, personal encounter with the divine.

Hildegard's story is not without its own irony. Although she attributes her voice to an external source apart from her own personality and wisdom, her writings introduce a positive view of women through the symbolic images of her visions. Four traditional female figures—Eve, Mary, Ecclesia, and Sapientia or Caritas—allow her to explore the natural experience of the feminine as an important dimension of the divine nature.[20] The Synagogue, for example, is a tall woman who, as the mother of the incarnation of the Word, carries in her arms and lap the prophets. This is a strong female image for a woman of words![21]

On the other hand, her writing readily reflects the traditional virtues of humility, obedience, and discretion that were central to the Benedictine community of which she was a part.[22] Although women's strength and experience is highlighted through her visions, Hildegard carefully included in the rhetoric of her interpretations the cultural assumptions that reinforced women's subservience. For instance, as she comments on the "fall of humanity" in Vision Two of the *Scivias*, she explains why the serpent chose to seduce Eve rather than Adam in the garden. She concludes with a blanket indictment of women in general, saying, "Thus woman very quickly overthrows man, if he does not hate her and accepts her words."[23] Here, her optimism about human ability is carefully subdued.

Through her moral teachings, Hildegard reinforced the established hierarchy among classes and genders, even though the symbols of her visions were radically inclusive and feminine. Using the analogy of the earth that cannot plow itself in order to produce fruit, she prohibits women from desiring the vocation of priesthood because their bodies are created to give birth physically and spiritually, like Mary the mother of Jesus. Thus, Hildegard reinforces the stereotypes of women perpetuated for centuries by the church.[24] Even so, she encouraged the women of her community not to brood over their unworthiness, but to be especially confident and joyful, to celebrate beauty on special holy days, and to wear pretty garments as an expression of their love for God.[25]

Hildegard of Bingen was an impressive woman of her time. Perhaps her entrance at an early age into a community of like-minded women gave her greater confidence in her own spiritual gifts and abilities. Perhaps her abnormal encounters with "fiery light" from an early age made her more sensitive and introspective, or made her feel "exceptional" in some way. Within the cultural context of the Middle Ages, however, her womanhood and her physiological episodes permitted her to claim a special weakness that made her more receptive to divine empowerment. Still, she sought and found approval from outside sources that encouraged her to exercise her gifts. Self-interest and self-knowledge that would stand in the way of becoming a "mouthpiece" for the divine voice were set aside in favor of the prophetic call and the mystical revelation she was commanded to write.

For the contemporary woman, Hildegard is somewhat of a paradox. Yet, her writings offer an alternative vision of God's nature for an ever-changing church. Her success as a mystic and a prophet can encourage those who are learning to trust their own voices through individual, spiritual union with God. The voice of the mystic can have an important mission for the wider community and world.

The Story of Louisa Mariah Layman Woosley

The emergence of women's voices in the Middle Ages was not paralleled or surpassed until the nineteenth century, when women began to express in a new way their experience of being called by God to preach. The evangelical fervor that erupted during the Second Great Awakening in America promoted personal religious experience as a source and standard for spiritual authority in the church. The appeal to repentance and faith was extended equally to both men and women. As a result, women often testified to an intense, personal relationship with God that initiated them into a new phase of self-identity and moral responsibility. If personal experience was an important standard for faith, it was difficult to deny that women were qualified to be spiritual authorities.[26]

This emphasis on personal and often emotional experience of God at that time provided a springboard for social movements that addressed concerns for human freedom and dignity. As members of the abolitionist, temperance, and missionary movements, women discovered their own ability to influence the moral climate of American life outside the private sphere through speaking and organizing for the work at hand.[27]

Women experienced the reality of resistance, as well. Lucretia Mott, a Quaker minister from Philadelphia, knew enormous personal freedom as a leader of the abolitionist movement in her area. When she traveled to London as a delegate to the World's Anti-Slavery Convention in 1840, the assembly refused to seat women as delegates, relegating them to the status of silent onlookers. Although Mott chose to remain silent in that assembly, she did not hesitate to preach in London churches. As a result, she won the admiration of Elizabeth Cady Stanton, who returned to America and led the movement for equal rights for women.[28]

Although Lucretia Mott enjoyed considerable freedom to speak within her own theological tradition, women in mainline denominations in America were met with strong resistance to their voices.[29] For example, the Presbyterian Church U.S.A., as early as 1826, posted warnings for ministers to guard against such innovations. The denomination continued to deny women ordination until 1956, when they changed their constitution to allow it.[30] Within other denominations, the ordination of women came sooner, but generally, it required engaging in ecclesiastical battles that were often brutal.

One of the earliest women preachers within the broader Presbyterian tradition in America was Louisa M. Woosley, a representative of women during the late nineteenth century who were called to preach within a strongly evangelical context.[31] She was ordained by Nolin Presbytery of the Cumberland Presbyterian Church on November 5, 1889. During the next twenty years she struggled within denominational structures over issues of freedom and authority in ministry. Finally, during a time of denominational crisis, the church returned her to a position of leadership and recognized the validity of her ordination in 1889. By 1921, when Woosley had reached the age of fifty-nine, the Cumberland Presbyterian Church chose to settle the "woman question" by reinterpreting its Confession of Faith and Constitution to be completely inclusive of both genders, bringing its official stance in line with the practice of its churches at that time.

Woosley was free to author her own story of conversion and call to ministry, but more extensively than Hildegard. She wrote and published a small volume containing a defense of women's ministry entitled *Shall Woman Preach? Or the Question Answered* in 1891.[32] After arguing extensively in favor of women's ministry from biblical, social, and theological perspectives, Woosley relates in the final chapter the story of the difficult struggle of finding voice as a woman preacher.

She tells the story of a woman, not of great privilege, but the daughter of a farmer within a rural district in central Kentucky. The cultural and theological conditioning of her father led him to deny his daughter further education beyond an elementary level. In a practice common to her times, she married when she was sixteen years of age and gave birth to two children within two years. Her husband, Curtis Woosley, was a farmer within the same county and a member of the Cumberland Presbyterian Church, which she joined after marrying him.

Louisa Woosley recalled having her first sense of calling at the age of twelve when she experienced conversion and baptism. She remembers being "impressed to labor in the vineyard of the Lord," but excused herself at the time because she considered herself too young, too uneducated, and too female. Having never heard of another woman preacher, she found it difficult to imagine such a vocation for herself.[33]

Her second wave of struggle came after her children were born. She had prayed that God would relieve her sense of responsibility by calling her husband to preach, instead of her. Her husband, however, was not so inclined. Unable to shake the persistent voice inside her, she turned to an authority within her tradition—the Bible. From the fall of 1882 to the spring of 1883 she read the complete canon, and afterward felt a greater sense of calling as a woman. Her own reading of the Bible had revealed how often God had chosen to work through women's lives and voices. [34]

Feeling imprisoned by cultural definitions of her role as a woman, Woosley continued to deny her call. Her inner voice cried out, "The people will not hear me, and I cannot get any work to do, and my husband will not be willing to let me go. My people [her family members] will dislike it!" She had excuses that would be accepted by the majority of people surrounding her, but the call persisted.

She was afraid to tell anyone about her desire to preach out of fear of rejection. Instead, she "kept it locked up in her heart." The psychological repercussion of this denial was enormous. She became extremely depressed, at times suicidal, and she began to doubt the authenticity of her relationship with God.

During that time, her young daughter, Vianna, had become gravely ill to the point of death. Woosley claimed responsibility for her daughter's illness because she had been unwilling to obey the voice of God. In contrition, Woosley promised God that she would respond. Soon her daughter recovered.

Still, she could not speak about her internal call. She rationalized that an uneducated woman could never find a place within the ranks of scholarly men. The strain of denial soon became unbearable for Woosley, and her physical health began to decline. By the spring of 1886, she was "reduced to a frame, and as helpless as an infant."[35] Finally, without enough strength to sit up in bed without assistance, Woosley accepted her experience of God's claim on her life. "I laid myself, my husband and two dear children upon God's altar, and with all my heart said, 'Oh Lord, lead me in a plain path, and show me thy way, that I may walk therein.'"[36]

Woosley's health improved dramatically in a matter of months. Still she told no one of her call. On January 1, 1887, the church session at her home church called on her to conduct the worship service in the absence of the regular pastor. This was her moment of truth. "By the help of God, I will do the best I can," she said and stepped into the pulpit for the first time to speak the message of God. A sense of peace rushed over her as she experienced the personal integrity that long had eluded her.[37]

The opposition that she had anticipated from those around her came crashing in. Friends of former days were now foes. Even her father withdrew from his relationship with her. The community thought her behavior was scandalous. But still she persisted. She had wrestled down her own internal doubts and fears in order to find peace with God. Her rejection by people who had held authority in her life was incredibly painful for her, but it could not compare with the years of internal suffering she had experienced until the call was answered.

At first she preached in outdoor meetings and in schoolhouses— wherever she could find people willing to listen. The Methodist Church provided a welcoming community for her gifts. Her success as an evangelist was so impressive, in fact, that members of her own denomination began to notice her. At that point, she was received as a candidate for ministry in the Cumberland Presbyterian Church and eventually ordained.[38]

Obviously, Woosley proved to be an effective speaker with a voice that appealed to the people. During her first four years of ministry she recorded having preached 912 sermons. Almost two thousand people had made some public faith response to her preaching, and more than five hundred were received as members of the Cumberland Presbyterian Church.[39]

Woosley lived a long, healthy life of service to the church. For more than thirty years, Woosley preached as an evangelist, traveling great distances for months at a time to hold extended meetings with various congregations. She was well over fifty years of age before reducing her workload and spending less time away from home. As her husband began to experience ill health, she developed pastoral relationships with congregations nearby and continued to preach regularly for over ten years. During her entire career, she was actively involved in the work of the denomination, serving as stated clerk of Leitchfield Presbytery for twenty-five years. Her extensive records reveal that within the course of forty-five years of ministry,

Woosley preached 7,925 sermons. Once she found her voice, she was never silent again.

The challenge of Woosley's call to speak was in reconciling her gender with her theological orientation. She knew that God had chosen her to speak for God, not as a hollow conduit for an alien word, but as a human being with a message for a particular context. Reconciliation came when she abandoned many self-imposed definitions of gender in order to take her place as an equal with men.

Her theological tradition made it possible for her to claim the authenticity of her call from God, even though women were not traditionally called. The leaders of her denomination considered the "secret internal call" of God absolutely essential for ministry, and they promoted that kind of experience through their preaching and teaching. Woosley's narrative of her call fits the classic model of the experiences claimed by many male preachers in her day, except that her excuses for resisting the call were related specifically to restrictions surrounding her gender, a struggle that none of her male counterparts could claim.

Woosley's extensive study of the Bible through the lens of her persistent call from God enabled her to affirm the right of all women to respond to God's desire for them to preach. She found her answers through common sense and expected the rest of the church to do the same. Her theology of redemption through Jesus Christ allowed her to challenge the theological assumptions about women's essentially evil natures. She claimed that the effectiveness of Christ's atonement had already made possible the redemption of fallen humanity, thereby restoring women to full and equal partnership with men. In addition, she applauded the work of the Holy Spirit, for whom gender did not seem to be an issue.

The evangelistic imperative of the late nineteenth and early twentieth centuries was incredibly optimistic about ushering in the "kingdom of God" on earth. Woosley shared that optimism and truly believed that through converting individuals to a saving knowledge of Jesus Christ, women's situation as a whole would be changed. Freedom from sin would result in the full restoration of equal rights between the sexes.

Woosley was one of many women who pioneered the frontier of women's ministry in mainline Protestant churches. As the first woman minister of her denomination, she was unique and exceptional in appearance and style. She defended her right as a woman to answer the call to preach in public ways. In her theology and preaching style, however, she communicated much like men. Her feminine voice used language and rhetoric that could be heard from male pulpits across the country. If she had only heard the voices of men proclaiming the word of God, how could she imagine any other sound? Would her voice have been acceptable to the general public if it had departed from the traditional homiletic style of her day? Voiced, yet silenced. The story of Louisa Woosley has its own irony, as well.

The Story of Beverly Wildung Harrison

Women who pioneered the second wave of American feminism in the 1970s and 1980s had to struggle to discover their authentic voices in much the same way as the women of earlier times. With the social structures being challenged by the voices of the civil rights movement, women's awareness of the sources of their silence began to broaden during this period. Women's understanding of their own oppression evolved. As a result, their consciousness expanded to include an awareness of the more subtle ways that women's authority was undermined by the culture in which they had been raised.

In an essay published in 1985, Beverly Wildung Harrison tells her story of coming to voice. She articulated an experience of having assumed a voice that was overly determined by others rather than one that articulated an authentic reflection of her own questions, a story that resonated with many women who were entering the ranks of the Protestant clergy during this formative period. Her naming of that experience has sparked recognition and growth for other women since that time.

In the essay "Keeping Faith in a Sexist Church: Not for Women Only,"[40] Harrison identifies herself as a survivor among the ranks of women who studied in theological seminaries in the 1950s and 1960s. Most became depressed, disillusioned, or discontent, and, thus, disappeared from ministry early on or remained clergy and did not seek active roles in ministry.

Harrison was born in 1932, during the Great Depression in the United States, into a "white, middle-strata family in a small Midwestern town, where women's roles were firmly fixed and where the influence of feminism had hardly permeated."[41] She grew up in an era when "feminism" was not spoken of in most spheres. Never hearing of the women who had struggled for basic rights, her consciousness was clouded by the expectations that all girls grew up to first seek to be wives and mothers, and perhaps later to work, if necessary. A family hardship turned out to be an asset for Harrison. Because her mother was widowed at an early age, with five children to support, Harrison was taught that women should be prepared to cope and, if need be, to be self-supporting. College education was acceptable and even desirable for women, although most did not expect to use their education in a lifelong career.

During the same period of time, Protestant churches were promoting an emphasis on ministry to youth. Denominational youth organizations allowed girls to assume some positions of leadership. Harrison found herself in a role as "perpetual vice-moderator" in the United Presbyterian Church. These experiences led her to gain a little confidence in her own leadership abilities.

Robert McAfee Brown, a scholar whom she admired, suggested that she study at Union Theological Seminary in New York. Other liberal male clergy echoed his encouragement, although they never imagined a role for her other than "Director of Christian Education." She entered seminary equipped with an interest in theology and an aspiration to serve the church. Once she arrived, she discovered that women actually pursued the standard ministerial degree programs that prepared clergy for ordination in the church.

Harrison decided to pursue a career in campus ministry, in large part because she had encountered another woman in that role, the Reverend Elizabeth Heller at the University of Minnesota. This had allowed her to imagine herself in that role, and fortunately, she had gifts that equipped her to succeed in that ministry. The thought of ordination was dismissed quickly. She explains: "I hardly made this decision consciously, however, because at that time I could not have tolerated the anxiety of sex role 'deviance,' not even in aspiration, much less in practice."[42] It was easier to identify with a female role model than to realistically assess her own distinctive gifts.

Upon graduation from seminary, Harrison took a job in campus ministry. She found herself supported by male colleagues who commended her ability to function in a style of ministry that they felt at home with. Their compliments included statements such as, "You are different from what we expected a woman to be," or "You *really* are good," or even "You are really one of the boys."[43] In other words, the subtle message communicated to her was that "because you are like us, that is, *not* like most women, we welcome you as a colleague."[44] During this time, she never particularly concerned herself with the issue of women's ordination that was being debated in the Presbyterian Church, considering that debate too "obvious" to address. She was accepted as a Commissioned Church Worker by San Francisco Presbytery, and she admits that she was out of touch with the struggle of other women to find supportive professional employment in the church.

How could a woman enter a career that had been systematically denied to persons of her gender without having some sensitivity to the
plight of women in general? Harrison explains:

> I realize now that I lived during these years with an internal
> psychic split that, given the times, was the cost of the acceptance
> by male peers that I so much valued. This split expressed itself in
> a deeply embedded uneasiness that I really must be *different* from
> other women, tougher, and, therefore, presumably less "feminine."
> Because I was acceptable to men and could operate in a "male
> mode," I felt inadequate as a woman. At the same time, male
> approval left me feeling superior to other women. A sense of
> superiority and a deep uneasiness that something was terribly
> wrong with me as a woman operated in my soul. As a result, my
> "success" cut me off from other women.[45]

Because of her "success" in ministry, she was encouraged to return to
graduate studies in theology. Toward the end of her Ph.D. work, Harrison
took a job as an assistant dean of students, with special responsibility for
women students. She found herself counseling women who were struggling with their own survival in seminary and in the church. Many of
them left seminary, and gave up aspirations for ministry. Harrison extended sympathy in their struggles but did not at first see a connection
between their disappointments, the loss to theological education, or her
own well-being.

As books and articles by radical feminists appeared in print, Harrison
began to listen to new voices that made her rethink the history of her
own development as a woman. As her story took new shape, the conversations with women students began to take on a new relevance and meaning
for her. Although the younger women were experiencing a clear call to
ministry, they did not fit the accepted norm. They needed freedom to
question, explore, and create new patterns for clergy. Slowly, Harrison
came to realize how her own conformity to external standards grew out
of a deeper sense of personal powerlessness, and that it had turned into
acts of sabotage for herself and for other women.

At the same time, she came to realize that each time she allowed
another woman to drift away from theological education, she was weak-
ening the base of support for her own work. She grew to understand that
she could not "live productively and well without those sisters" and that
she "needed the enhanced environment of support their presence and
creativity offered."[46]

As she began to support and advocate for the ministry of other women, Harrison began to discover her own voice. She realized how much authority she had given to the external voices around her, suspending her own freedom and escaping her own personal issues. She began to ask new questions about her own beliefs. As she began to identify and claim the theological issues that really mattered to her, Harrison found a new clarity in her thinking.

Of course, she also experienced new resistance from a number of colleagues, including some who had once given her support. It had never occurred to her that her "cautiousness and restraint, born of ambivalence, had been a source of some of the affirmation that she had received."[47]

Harrison's personal story continues to unfold. Since coming to voice as a feminist, Harrison has gained a wide reputation as a spokesperson for many social concerns, including the rights of gays and lesbians. She has served many years as the Carolyn Williams Beard Professor of Christian Ethics at Union Theological Seminary in New York. Her areas of research and teaching expertise include methods for social ethics, feminist theology, intimate and domestic violence, and sexual and economic ethics.

Although this story about Harrison recounts only the early years of her ministry, it illustrates the importance of personal authenticity as a factor in coming to voice. What if she had continued to accept for herself the external standards that assured the support of many male clergy? Would her success have allowed her to win acceptance for other women entering ministry, or would it have made it more difficult for them to be accepted? How would the resulting internal, psychic tension have manifested itself? Harrison finally resolved these issues so that her own voice and the voices of other women could be fully valued. She has made peace with her own vocation in the church, and as a result, has made meaningful contributions to the life of the world. For women who enter a career in ministry today, however, the sound of these questions may still ring true. Personal authenticity is still a crucial issue for women in ministry.

Echoes

These four stories of women's voices bring together various contexts. Each woman experienced her faith within a different historical moment. Each dealt with cultural definitions of her freedom and responsibility. Each came to faith within a particular church community that understood itself within the philosophical and theological worldview of the time. Each had a different set of experiences that shaped her development. And yet, each of these women found a voice to articulate an experience of faith. Their voices have been preserved to echo in the contemporary moment. Through their expression, we find meaning for our own stories today.

Imagine what might happen if these four women gathered together around a table to discuss their understanding of voice. The conversation, with the aid of interpreters, probably would be alive with staccatos of disagreement and crescendos of alarm as the women explored their experiences from radically different worldviews. On the other hand, their struggle to exercise faith, strength, and commitment to their vocations might bring harmony into the discussion. Could it be that if these women sat down together to discuss "voice," a deeper sense of "knowing" would take shape among them? If you believe in the importance of the human voice, the answer would have to be "yes!"

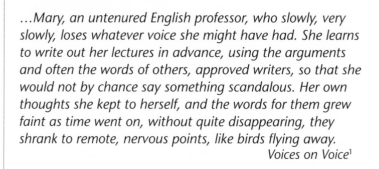

...Mary, an untenured English professor, who slowly, very slowly, loses whatever voice she might have had. She learns to write out her lectures in advance, using the arguments and often the words of others, approved writers, so that she would not by chance say something scandalous. Her own thoughts she kept to herself, and the words for them grew faint as time went on, without quite disappearing, they shrank to remote, nervous points, like birds flying away.

Voices on Voice[1]

Women are only now beginning to uncover our own truths, many of us would be grateful for some rest in that struggle, would be glad not to lie down with the shards we have painfully unearthed, and be satisfied with these. Often I feel this like an exhaustion in my own body.

Adrienne Rich[2]

...no person is your friend (or kin) who demands your silence, or denies your right to grow and be perceived as fully blossomed as you were intended. Or who belittles in any fashion the gifts you labor so to bring into the world.

Alice Walker[3]

You were silent for so long....

Mom

Chapter 6

To Be Saved from Silence

The women of the New Testament, the Middle Ages, the nineteenth century, and the present day bring something important to a theology of speaking and preaching that is born in a climate of resistance. In their own ways, the stories of these women demonstrate how the human voice can penetrate even the most pervasive systems of silencing and oppression. Their voices were heard. Their voices were remembered.

At first glance it would seem that the contemporary woman is fortunate; she does not live in such a climate, an atmosphere where her words and presence are not valued. After all, we are the heirs of the advances of the feminist and womanist movements. Clearly in the past three decades women have witnessed the publication of *Ms.* magazine, and women have made their importance felt in the workplace. New occupations have opened their doors. In the theological world, there has been an explosion of the publication of feminist commentaries on biblical texts. A few years ago, both the quantity and quality of these texts could not have been predicted. Alternative feminist christologies have been formulated. Women's studies programs have drawn a diverse group of students. We have lived through the Decade of Women. Seminaries are filled with women, young and not so young, now free to explore through higher education their faith systems and callings. Women have found some first, small congregations willing, at least temporarily, to "try them out."

And yet, as evidenced in the stories of the women clergy who gathered with us "around the table" in our theological institutions, the picture is not as clear and unambiguous as it first may seem. This is the age where women's reproductive choice is still a heated political issue. A prominent denomination issues a statement on the woman's place in the home. Unresolved debates are still raging over inclusive language and the ordination of women to the priesthood. There is a heightened awareness of the desperate plight of women around the world who have so few choices. Sexism is still rampant, but perhaps more subtle than in generations past and, thus, much more dangerous. Land mines are invisible, waiting to explode. The world may be deceived into thinking that women's finding voice is no longer a troubling or urgent concern, and yet, it is very urgent. As a student at PSR once wrote, "If you're not alarmed, you just aren't paying attention."

Virginia Woolf, in "Professions for Women," published in 1942, describes what it is like to go against the grain of internalized dominant cultural voices or to try to write while the "Angel in the House" hovers over her shoulder, whispering all the cultural messages about what women are supposed to be and do. Woolf's angel told her, "...never let anyone know you have a mind of your own. Had I not killed the angel," Woolf said, "she would have killed me." We would like desperately to believe that the cultural voices that threatened to drown the voice of Virginia Woolf have been silenced. Sadly that is not so. The subtle, invisible warping of thought that occurs in the imaginations of women continues to take its toll on women's esteem and their abilities to define and describe life in any authoritative way.

How do we silence the voice of the angel? How do we defend against cultural messages—that institutionalized negation that often operates unchallenged behind our backs? That is the question Virginia Woolf asked. How do we find the voice of our own?[4] Has it been lost?

Several studies have been conducted in order to understand women's experience. In two specific studies, women were interviewed and observed in an effort to discern their ways of knowing authority, both other's and their own. These findings are instructive for our purposes because they are focused clearly around the metaphor of voice. Replete with women's narratives and punctuated with observations and conclusions about contemporary women, these studies examine and highlight issues of voice, authority, relationship, and power. They are essential for understanding ourselves as people, as preachers.

In their recent work *Meeting at the Crossroads,* Brown and Gilligan outline what seems to be an inevitable process, one in which adolescent girls give up voice and abandon self. Their research records and reflects upon the voices of nearly one hundred girls between 1986 and 1990. Evidence revealed that, as the girls approached adolescence, they began to struggle to take seriously their own voices in conversation and respond to their own thoughts and feelings. They exhibited increased confusion, sometimes defensiveness. Their clarity, courage, and connectedness became compromised. Living in a male-voiced culture and male-governed society encouraged the girls to make a debilitating move toward silence; they demonstrated that the passage out of girlhood is a journey into disconnection, a troubled crossing, when a girl loses a firm sense of self and becomes tentative and unsure. There is evidence of a loss of voice, a struggle to authorize or take seriously her own experience. [5]

Contradiction emerges. As women silence themselves to avoid separation from others, they create separation of another kind by becoming divorced from their own desires and feelings. The separation is from the truest self, and the connection in relationship becomes a kind of false intimacy. One after another, the girls moving into adolescence struggled to hold onto their own experience, to know what they knew, to speak in their own voices, to bring their own knowledge into the world in which they lived. There was the fear that one's experience, if ever spoken, would endanger relationships and threaten survival.

An Asian American woman sent me a quote that comes out of her own cultural context: 'She who knows, doesn't speak. She who speaks, doesn't know.' Does this tell you something about silence?

MDT

The tragedy came upon them quietly and subtly. Like a thief in the night, someone or something came in and robbed them of a positive sense of self. They developed, unbeknownst to themselves, a "no-voice voice." Woolf's "angel," they discovered, is still with us.

This study is just one of many that look at the crisis of the adolescent girl in our society. Despite the feminist movement and gains made by women in home, academy, and workplace, the alarming trend among adolescent girls continues, if not intensifies. The flood of research is both statistical and narrative in nature. Peggy Orenstein in *School Girls: Young Women, Self Esteem, and the Confidence Gap* illustrates vividly the "free fall" in self-esteem and confidence that adolescent girls experience. Many fall into the traditional patterns of low self-image, doubt, and self-censorship of their creative and intellectual potential. These girls emerge from adolescence with reduced expectations; they are more vulnerable to feeling depressed and hopeless. Girls are much more likely than boys to say they are "not smart enough" or "not good enough" to achieve their dreams.[6] Mary Pipher, in *Reviving Ophelia: Saving the Selves of Adolescent Girls,* describes America today as "a Girl-Destroying Place." She searches for ways that we can encourage daughters to be independent and autonomous, and still keep them safe.[7]

To talk about this process in a group of women usually prompts some of them to remember the exact moment in their own growing up years when they felt the world silence them, or when they began to silence themselves. Others often cannot remember an exact time, an exact experience, but when looking back, they can see that, yes, voice was taken from them or they had given it away. They are left to wonder, "When did that happen?" The "angel" is still with us.

This process takes place, and often it does not naturally or easily reverse itself. This is demonstrated in the research of Belenky, Clinchy, Goldberger, and Tarule who interviewed a diverse group of women in an effort to determine what they know and how they know it.[8] They focused on the development of voice. The researchers organized the women into five categories. In the first two, women had little, if any, ability to claim some sense of authority, and their agency was curtailed. In yet another category, women could trust only their own experience; the women trusted themselves and only themselves. In the last two categories, women were able to synthesize their own thoughts and feelings with those of others.

I realize how powerful words are to young people when adults speak. You can silence, disparage them. At camp I told about being a teenager, pregnant and not married. After I did, the young girls began to talk about their own difficult personal issues. The reason I told the story is because it was a time of silence for me. I was silenced by disappointed families, my dad's authority, a world without abortion, and my own fear. I needed someone to talk to. Voice equals choice and voice equals freedom. I think of that new world as my ministry—to create a safe place for young women to be voiced.

AS

The difficulty some women have in valuing their own thoughts and emotions attests to the sometimes nearly imperceptible process by which women internalize the dominant forces in the world that have rejected or oppressed them. From infancy on, women are discouraged in many ways from speaking out or claiming their voice. The discouragement is successful when women internalize the cultural messages and silence themselves. Despite the feminist movement, it is evident that this mechanism continues to operate. Entrenched values are powerful and highly resistant to change. The result is that these women may experience a loss of self-esteem, depression, outrage, anxiety, and loneliness.[9]

Oppression is both an external and an internal reality.[10] Think about the constellation of feelings that can result from living in a world where one is not valued. **Shame**—the painful feeling arising from being dishonorable, improper. **Disgrace**—feeling unsightly, to feel inferior by comparison. **Fear**—feeling distressed because of some impending pain or danger. **Guilt**—feeling remorse for some real or imagined offense. These feelings work to silence the woman as she begins to think that her contributions to the world are not valuable, are inferior.[11] She may begin to believe that if she speaks, she will experience harm. As women fail to hear themselves speak, they are unable to sustain the convictions and feelings of "I" and self. Instead, they sink into self-doubt about the legitimacy of their privately held experience. Women sacrifice genuine intimacy where the fullest self is brought into the relationship. Self and voice become the price paid for acceptability.[12]

It is not surprising that strong and disempowering cultural messages find powerful expression among women who have been called to preach. What happens, then, when the woman called to preach has lost her voice at adolescence and not yet found it? What happens when a woman called to preach has internalized the notion that her life experience holds no authority? What if she believes the myth that her thinking is inferior and her emotions prevent her from being in the world in a serious and productive way? What happens when God calls this woman to stand in the pulpit and speak a word to the gathered community?

Tradition silences people in the islands. Only men could preach. But in the early '80s, the Free Wesleyan women started preaching. Lately, people are going overseas to study, and they come back with new ideas about women.

OL

The Church Colludes

At first glance, it is ironic that the church has embraced society's notion of women. Yet, it is true. Cultural oppression has been embraced by a church that teaches women "not to speak," because women's speech is considered not only counter-cultural, it is taught to be "counter-God." How could this happen when the texts we embrace seem to hold such a powerful liberating impulse? We read that female and male alike were created in the likeness of the Creator and called forth to create the good and dispel the bad through speech. Why should that view of women's power not be believed?

Another look at the biblical text, however, reveals the persistent ambiguity of the message women have received from this tradition. In the story of the exodus and wilderness wanderings, we come across powerful and contradictory images of women as the Israelites make their way from oppression to freedom. On the one hand, we have the daughters of Zelophehad—Mahlah, Noah, Hoglah, Milcah, and Tirzah. (Numbers 27:1–11) Traveling with Moses through the wilderness, they approach the great Moses, the priest, the leaders, and the entire congregation. Gathering courage, perhaps from each other's presence, they give voice to the inequity they found in the God-given law. "Our father died in the wilderness," they said, "and he had no sons." They wonder why the father's property should go only to male heirs. They demanded that Moses give them their rightful possession. Moses brought their case before Yahweh. And Yahweh replies, "They are right..." The law was forever changed.

Juxtaposed to this picture of forthrightness is the picture of Miriam who, along with her brother Aaron, dares to challenge Moses. They ask, "Has the Lord spoken only through Moses? Has he not spoken through us also?" Yahweh calls Miriam and Aaron forward and asks them why they were not afraid to speak against the servant Moses. Yahweh's anger is kindled, and when Yahweh departs, Miriam has become leprous, white as snow.

Forceful sisters speak, and the law is changed. A woman asks a question about authority; she is stricken unclean and for seven days is put outside the camp. The confusion of this theological dilemma is compounded by the "redemption" of Miriam in Micah 6 and in rabbinic literature where her leprosy is healed and her great beauty is restored.

In the New Testament story of Luke-Acts Anna and Mary speak as prophets, as do the four daughters of Philip (Acts 21:9). Mary learns from Jesus the teacher (Luke 10), and Priscilla teaches. Yet, when the women face the empty tomb and embrace the mission to tell the disciples what they have seen, "the story seemed like nonsense, and they refused to believe them." Women are taught by Jesus and speak for Jesus. They pray and they prophesy. Yet, even so visibly embraced, welcomed, challenged, and given the task of proclamation, the world will not listen.

Riddled with ambiguity in text and tradition, Christianity has silenced its women, or

My grandfather was not silent, but when it came down to the final analysis, my grandmother's words were God's voice, the guiding voice. That same woman, however, would not have the same authority in her position in the church. She and other women were teachers, principals of schools. Yet, they were silent in the church.   *RN* has tried, punishing them if they should ask a question about authority. It would not be surprising if women called to speak out in the church should have opted for flight or silence. It would not be surprising that they should experience doubt, shame, disgrace, fear, guilt, inferiority, and isolation. These are demons of mind and spirit.

Our history as a church is blessed, however, with stories of women who, empowered by God's spirit, have courageously chosen to speak rather than to flee. We can trace a feminist presence in the church back to the very foundations of our nation, and sense its tenacious, resilient spirit embedding itself in the bones and surviving despite all attempts to dispel or destroy it.[13]

Yet, in each generation, feminist work is received as if it had no historical past. It seems "orphaned." The work of feminists seems to lack a tradition.[14] Accomplished women are often misunderstood and then forgotten. Elizabeth Cady Stanton and Susan B. Anthony worked closely with each other to hammer out political strategy and speeches. They organized meetings, and often, together, suffered indignities and abuse. When Stanton died, reporters interviewed Anthony, her closest friend and colleague. The questions revealed that the reporters knew little about their work. In dismay, Anthony asked, "How shall we ever make the world knowledgeable of our movement?"[15] How can the history of struggle and progress be transmitted for the benefit of women in the present day?

In our own day, many women are still at a loss as to how to deal with the disempowering aspects of the church and its structures of authority. Controlled leadership and oppressive language are two manifestations of this resistance to women's power. Hear these words of women recorded by the authors of *Defecting in Place,* a volume that chronicles the experiences of many women in faith traditions. Many of these women stay somehow involved in organized religious communities, and yet look elsewhere, perhaps to newer emerging communities, to meet their spiritual needs.

Those of us who, in whatever respects, haven't been embraced by the institutional church know that the institution isn't going to do anything for us. Our authority is more spiritually driven: I'm doing this because God's telling me to do it. That is so threatening. That's the piece that feels so controversial and scary, so I put a blanket on it. People are threatened when they think that you aren't beholden to them in an institutional way. You become sort of a wild card; they haven't given you anything, so they can't take anything away. CC

I feel more often than I should, "silenced," not because I am not free to speak, but because I am not fully heard.[16]

As a Roman Catholic woman, I live with the pain of belonging to a church institution probably unparalleled in its structural sexism and its commitment to an authoritative hierarchy (and too often an implicit theology) that is exclusive and oppressive. I have felt silenced, ignored, invisible, unimportant.[17]

It is difficult for many women to speak out—or even think out.[18]

The struggle women face in the church is a reflection of the struggle we see on a more cosmic scale of entrenchment in systems—economic, political, etc., that no longer work and in fact are destructive. The stakes are high around this issue, for our very survival is reflected in it, as a people, as a planet.[19]

I will not believe in a God who does not believe in me.[20]

The problem is twofold. On the one hand, women often feel that their needs and thoughts are not valued in the life of the ecclesial community. Many can attest to being ignored, rendered invisible in meetings, both in local and national settings; to being bombarded with curious looks; to being overlooked for parishes where the community "is just not ready" for female leadership. To compound the problem, church leaders are not speaking out about the issue, further isolating and stigmatizing those women who feel compelled to speak out on behalf of themselves. Silence in the area of women's issues in the church and in society is a scandalous sin of omission for many clergy.[21]

The church originally looked to the ministry of Jesus of Nazareth for its vision and identity. While there is disagreement about his acceptance of women and how countercultural his actions were for his day, the gospels do remember a person who noticed those "on the fringes" of society. Jesus modeled inclusivity and equality for all people. Especially radical, perhaps, was his respect for women and his treatment of them as valuable participants in furthering the realm of God on earth. How- ever, the church was unable to sustain such a countercultural reality for an extended period of time. The church became more patriarchal as it debated

> The strongest voice in my church is a woman's.
> SLK

the question of women's authority. Since that time, patriarchy has been sustained by the church through a variety of devices.[22] Male domination has been particularly true in the arena of preaching. Historically the preacher has been considered a messenger of God, or as the one speaking God's word. As Word, God has traditionally been prevented from being represented by woman; woman has been often been profiled as taboo.[23] It has been difficult for the church to believe that the Word might come from the voices, the bodies, of women.[24]

To deny women authority is not only to render them speechless but also to truncate their psychological, intellectual, and emotional development. Theological underpinnings for the undermining of women's voice and authority are set within limits of how the church has used language for God that is exclusively male. People who live in a minority status may find that the language taught by dominant culture fails to fit their experience of reality. Without language to match their experience, persons may live in a choked silence, without any "voice." For women growing up in a patriarchal culture, attempting to describe their experiences through language may come across as a "lie" rather than as authentic expression. In fact, the original "voice" that might express the authentic self of a person may be suffocated by the confines of the "language world" she or he is given. One woman explains her experience of language in this way: "I had no words. I paused. I stuttered. I could find no word in the English language that could express my emotion. But I had to speak." In such cases it takes great effort to move beyond the framework of reality created by the "conservators" of language. It can be done, however, if the will to claim one's own experience overpowers the stronghold of dominant structures. In such cases, one must seek out new language to express oneself or find the space and time to reconstruct a new framework out of old timbers of the language one has been given. Such is the contemporary search of the woman in the church—looking for new theological language, new liturgical language to describe her experience of life, love, God, salvation, redemption, joy as true and good.

Many have studied the effects of theological language on women and the thoughts they generate in women about themselves in relation to the world. Carroll Saussy explores what she sees to be a contradiction in the life of faith: "I have been particularly curious about the conflict between religious faith's claims about a God of love and the believer's inability to love themselves."[25] She concludes that there is a correlation between women's self-esteem and their images for God. It is difficult for women to develop a "good enough" self-esteem when their "religious worldview" is that women are not equal to men nor created in God's image.

This situation of women in the church raises interesting questions. What happens when the woman who has been marginalized in the church is called to preach? What happens when she finds barriers to her ministry at so many turns? What happens when a woman is called to preach within the church that has denied her experience by refusing to hear her language, her experiences, or her new understandings of God? How can women, in the face of oppression, understand that our coming to voice as preachers is part of God's good purpose? Where do we seek the courage and the stamina to speak? One historic voice offers us an answer.

The Singing Something

In 1858, Anna Julia Cooper was born in Raleigh, North Carolina. Her mother, a slave and her father, her mother's master, Anna became one of the most highly educated and intellectual black women of her century. Teacher, administrator and scholar, Cooper received her Ph.D. at the Sorbonne. Her dissertation was entitled "Attitudes toward Slavery in Revolutionary France."

Like other prestigious black women of her time, she sought to implement a vision of freedom and justice. It was through her *A Voice from the South,* published in 1892, that Cooper questioned and challenged the domination of the weak by the strong in our culture. She attacked the evils of domination as they were made manifest in racism, sexism, and classism.

Dr. Cooper's work is important and striking because she recognized so early the importance of the woman's voice, and she thought about this voice from a theological perspective. In one of her pamphlets, she metaphorically described God's presence in humanity as a divine spark, a shadow mark, an urge cell. Most interesting, however, is her designation of God as a "Singing Something." This "Singing Something" is the movement toward freedom and equality in the human being that rises up against domination. God acts as a

I have had more "out of body experiences" singing than I have had preaching. I often talk about my voice as an instrument unto herself. She is her own being and when she feels like singing, she sings. I'm just standing there and she decides to utter. In singing, you have to listen—to the musician, to the audience, to yourself—but in a way that is not self-serving. It is just listening, listening for the voice.

RN

liberating voice and as an author of reform through that movement within human beings.

Through her love for music, Cooper came to use musical terminology to describe the importance of coming to speech. Blacks, she noted, were like a muffled chord. The black woman was a mute and voiceless note. Interestingly, black women were considered open-eyed, but silent. Aware of the oppression that stifled their creativity and fullness, Cooper maintained that the black woman's "little Voice" must be added to the chorus. The voice might be first heard as a lament, perhaps nothing but a cry. It might be broken utterances, but it would not be in vain. It was repressive, Cooper thought, for one half of the human family (the female half) to be stifled. As a result, the world only perceives half-truths.

For Cooper, then, being created in God's likeness is not imagistic. It is musical and auditory. Cooper understood our god-likeness to be in sound, words, voice. Thus, she spoke of not being created in the *image* of God, but in the *sound* of God. This distinguishes the sacredness of the human spirit as a kind of energy and force that moves body to action. Through voice, one asserts one's sacredness and beauty.[26]

Voice: Redemptive and Prophetic

What does it mean for those to preach who have been silenced and marginalized from the pulpit? For Cooper, silence was something to be saved from. This required courageous action, emboldened action on her part. She had to struggle against seemingly insurmountable obstacles. Being saved from her silence meant resistance and faith. Like the lamenter in the Psalms who through speech is drawn into new life, so it is for those who have been silenced and for those who have been marginalized from the pulpit.

When a person who has been oppressed and silenced stands and speaks, that person experiences redemption. It is a redemptive moment because it relies on grace and moves toward wholeness. It moves us toward our god-likeness. The internal movement is from fear to faith, shame to acceptance, guilt to forgiveness, denial to affirmation. Indeed, it is from dis/ grace to grace, and thus it is mysterious and sacramental. God-likeness is drawn forth from the Singing Something within.[27] Moving from silence into speech for any oppressed, colonized, or exploited being is healing. At the same time, this gesture of defiance makes new life possible[28] It is liberation.

And what does it mean to stand in the pulpit to speak? To stand in the pulpit to speak is not only redemptive, but prophetic. When the woman stands to speak, she embodies the inclusive, spirit-filled nature of the word. She fulfills her God-given nature to be created in the sound of one who brought the earth into being through speech, creating goodness. By her very presence a new world is drawn out of the old. The old is destroyed, plucked up, turned over. The new is built. It is a creative act of justice and inclusivity. It breaks barriers. As Rebecca Chopp says, "When a woman stands to preach, proclamation leaves its ecclesial prison."[29]

It is not easy of course. As Audre Lorde confessed, "I have come to believe over and over again that what is most important to me must be spoken, made verbal and shared, even at the risk of having it bruised or misunderstood."[30] Prophets encounter resistance, resentment, misunderstanding. Thus, there is a constant bind for those called to preach, yet barred from the pulpit. They must consistently prove themselves worthy (to both themselves and others) of the rights others take for granted. It is a constant battle within and without. Often the prophet calls members of a community to come to terms with the "other," to reassess thoughts, feelings, actions toward those who are different from themselves.

> The stepping into the role of ministry by a woman of Asian heritage is a prophetic act. It's breaking the expectation of the tradition. It is going against the grain.
>
> COD

For a woman called to preach, the prophetic act may be to come to terms with self—coming to understand that she is enough. As Richard Thulin says, "I am... deeply saddened when some female students tell me that they have no life-stories worth telling."[31] Overcoming the messages of society that tell her that she has nothing to offer, she must struggle to stand and resist the symbols, words, and ecclesiastical structures that limit her full participation in the reign of God . She must find courage to speak authentically and distinctively from her own life experience.[32]

There are many reasons why people justify and advocate for women's preaching. For some it is reasonable and in accordance with an understanding of the equality of all who are created. Some believe that women bring a distinctive word that is more relational, imaginative, nurturing, personal, and concrete. They believe that the community will hear a new dimension of the gospel when it is proclaimed by women. And then, still others turn to the analysis of social systems, arguing that structures that discriminate on the basis of sex, race, class, ethnic origin, sexual orientation are in conflict with the gospel.[33] Perhaps there is some truth in all of these positions, and more.

The "rightness" of women standing to preach must have something to do with the sound of God, the bringing forth of what was given to us at the moment of our creation. It witnesses to the ability of all human beings to make expression in the world and to the call to live intimately in covenant with a listening and speaking God. This God longs for us also to listen and to speak words formed and fashioned from the *ruach,* God's very breath. Not only are women disenfranchised when not allowed to speak, so are men and our children, who end up with unquestioned and skewed views of reality.

In their comprehensive study of women clergy, the authors Zikmund, Lummis, and Chang indicate that it may even be **more** difficult for today's women graduating from seminary and finding their way into ministry than for those several decades before. Today's women, they indicate, may be less capable of coping with sexism in the church. Clergywomen who attended seminary in the 1970's identified themselves as "pioneers" and knew that they had to develop strengths and coping strategies to survive and make a difference in the system. They knew that they were "going first." But for those who came later, there was a belief that the worst forms of discrimination were over; they did not recognize situations that were biased against them. Discrimination less glaring and struggles less public led them to believe that barriers were down, and the pioneer spirit faded. Women graduates now are more likely to feel that personal progress and success is more dependent upon their own merit and worth than on systemic change. They are more likely to blame themselves for failure.[34]

Echoes

You can't always see them, you can't always hear them. But they are there—massive and entrenched forces that silence. From infancy on, women are discouraged in many, many ways from speaking out or from finding and claiming voice. The discouragement is successful when women internalize the cultural messages and silence themselves. Despite the feminist movement, it is evident from studies on adolescent girls that these mechanisms continue to operate and find a home in many women who have been called to preach.

A woman who preaches, then, is working against these vast forces, although her preaching may not be seen as such. Consequently, she may experience doubt, shame, inferiority, and isolation. She must face and vanquish these feelings. Even so, her own grief and despair will become part of that which is spoken and remembered. To speak out, then, becomes a courageous act. Voice, especially woman's voice, becomes prophetic and redemptive when viewed in the midst of a resistant environment designed to silence it. In the midst of the struggle, God is faithful. Doubts and fears can be transformed into prophetic presence.

I go to the chapel for silence, for guidance, for language. The granite gravity of tradition crushes even the simplest of images. I cannot breathe, let alone think of preaching. Phrases of men who lectured here drift and rustle in piles. Why don't you speak up?

Marge Piercy[1]

Over twenty years after the second wave of feminism swept ashore in North America, patriarchy—with all its attendant dualistic hierarchies of winners and losers, dominant and marginalized, powerful and powerless—continues to hold the beach against all comers.

Mary Ann Tolbert[2]

When language is no longer related to silence, it loses its source of refreshment and renewal and therefore something of its substance...By taking it away from silence, we have made language an orphan.

Max Picard[3]

Listening is the beginning, silence is the hearing.

Nelle Morton[4]

Chapter 7

Coming to Voice

As women enter ministry, a transfer of value from an understanding of "Word" to "voice" can affect how we think about both the nature of preaching and preacher. It creates a crisis and a dilemma.

Hermeneutical theories suggest that the reader of the biblical text participates in the creation of its meaning. The interpreter is part of a conversation, a dialogue, in which she engages her own thought with text, tradition, and the world. Exegetical theories lead us to understand that we are to come to the text with a "suspicion" that allows us to filter out oppressive textual tendencies. Homiletic theory underscores the fact that we address a particular and distinctive community; our word to them may not be like the word brought elsewhere. Narrative theory suggests that story has multiple meanings, even a "surplus" of them. Feminist and womanist theory cautions us that the biblical text was not written by women, does not engage the world of women except to silence it, and that to find a liberating place there, women must come to the text with forceful challenge, strong questions, and imagination. These work together in ways that demand that the preacher bring forth the gospel in her own distinctive, authentic, authoritative, resistant, and relational voice, born of spirit and expressive of one's own god-likeness. The voice of the preacher, in its own distinctive form and register, is a place where God becomes present. Voice contextualizes word and allows for plurality. Voice is the point of integration between word, world, and self.

We have come to understand that our culture silences the woman and stifles her ability to know and express both thought and feeling. At a time when preaching demands *self*, for many it cannot be found. For those who have learned to survive in the world by losing voice, the journey to the pulpit is fraught with seemingly insurmountable obstacles. Self-doubt ushers in the plaguing question: What do I have to offer the gathered community? What if the preacher has long forgotten how to formulate her own thought, and what if she has learned not to trust her own heart? What if the message of the church is that her "voice" is not valued or welcomed there? Such is the experience of the one silenced and marginalized from the pulpit—yet called to preach. *Such is the one who needs to be saved from silence.*

This is where the learning of preaching must begin—not with homiletic style but with "unlearning not to speak," learning to trust one's own voice so that the sermon can be "populated with one's own accent." In writing of Saint Catherine of Siena, one author has said that she did what human beings have regularly done when confronted by forces that they cannot control, forces that would crush them or stunt them or strip them bare. They have used their imaginations. Imagination for these women is the vital component of resistance, for it allows them to hold on to a positive view of themselves no matter what the world tells them they are.[5] It is in stimulating this imagination that preaching begins.

The Imagining

It was the first day of the introductory class in preaching at PSR. Eleven women sat in the circle. Their bodies were stiff and their backs pressed tightly against their chairs. There was some nervous laughter and some quiet chatter. They knew each other; many of them knew each other well. But this was the first time that the ten of them had gathered for their introductory class in preaching. All were second-or third-year seminary students, and some of them (maybe two) had even preached a sermon before. But for most of the ten students who gathered there with the professor, standing behind the pulpit to speak a word to the gathered community was not yet a part of their own life experience. Some were not sure they wanted it to be.

The first assignment in the class was for each woman to come with a written statement

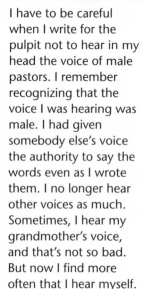

I have to be careful when I write for the pulpit not to hear in my head the voice of male pastors. I remember recognizing that the voice I was hearing was male. I had given somebody else's voice the authority to say the words even as I wrote them. I no longer hear other voices as much. Sometimes, I hear my grandmother's voice, and that's not so bad. But now I find more often that I hear myself.

RN

entitled "Imagining Myself as a Preacher." What do you see, Mary asked them, when you imagine yourself there in front of the community of faith? What do you hear?

The reflections of the women the next week were not surprising, but as each woman spoke, the group was overwhelmed by the enormous amount of fear and excitement that the preaching task held. One student, as she imagined herself standing behind the pulpit, saw looming over her head the many male preachers in her childhood, their index fingers pointed at her and shaking. She then saw the face of the male preacher who welcomed her into the church as an adult and gave her an unprecedented understanding of love and grace. When she tried to imagine herself speaking, however, there was nothing. There was not a word.

The next student described herself as small, dwarfed by a large wooden pulpit. She was wearing a heavy robe and stole, so heavy that it rendered her powerless. Her arms could not be lifted. Others, when trying to imagine themselves as preacher, could not see themselves there at all. The pulpit was vacant, and the room was filled with a deafening silence.

The conversation sparked by these "imaginings" had several dominant themes. Some could not see themselves in the pulpit because they had rarely seen a woman there. Some wondered if they had anything of value to say. Others wondered, even if they became experienced preachers, if the church community would accept them. Would they be discounted or excluded? Would they be reduced to silence? One, trusting the members of the group, spoke of her conflicted feelings about women and preaching. Should a woman speak "the word of the Lord?" All ten of them were filled with anticipation. Ten Protestant women were beginning to wrestle with the personal implications of the Word and their own words.[6] Did they have anything of value to say?

Mary left the classroom wondering how she could help them. How could she "hear these women into speech"? She went back to her office and sat at the computer, typing out the following memo to send to each:

I was awkward. I would stand with my legs off balance, not gesturing, looking down. I was doing things I wouldn't let myself get by with as a public speaker. I was doing little girl things, like you watch a fifth grader do when she's nervous. What was the problem? I didn't know exactly what my voice sounded like in the pulpit. That was what my body and my behavior were telling me. I was insecure. The issue? Authority. Lack of trust in my own voice.

CC

Do You Know Something About:
Joy
Sadness
Suffering
Grace
Betrayal
The pain of betraying
Doubt
Healing
Comfort
Longing
Giving
Anger
Hurt
Frustration
Selfishness
Grief
Loss
Hope
Surprise
Challenge
Love
Disappointment
Gratitude????????
THEN YOU HAVE SOMETHING TO SAY FROM THE
PULPIT!

Women must believe in their own experience before they can believe in their voices.[7]

As the semester progressed, the class discussed exegetical method,
hermeneutical methodologies, theologies of preaching, and sermon form.
Finally the day came when the first student was to preach her sermon.
The preacher was pale, clutching the sermon manuscript in trembling
hands. Before she stood to speak, Mary read to the group several stories,
one an excerpt from the memories of Rebecca Jackson, an A.M.E. preacher
in the early nineteenth century:

In 1835, I was in the West. I thought I would not mention this
but I feel it a duty to do so—persecution was raging on every
side. The Methodist ministers told the trustees not to let me speak

in the church nor any of the houses. And nobody must go to hear me—if they did, they should be turned out of the church. This great persecution throwed open doors for me. Even a wicked drunken man, when the members was afraid to let me speak in their houses and the people wanting to hear *the word, he opened his house and said,* "Let her come into my house and preach. I don't belong to meeting." So when the people heard, they came and told me. I went. The house was filled and all around the house and the road each way.[8]

Mary's audience was a community of female preachers, overwhelmed by the dedication of this woman who felt her calling so strongly that the oppression of the church couldn't stop her, a woman who would preach both "in spite of" and "because of." Was there no fear within her? Was she never pale? Did her hands ever tremble? Mary read on.

And at this time, I had as much upon me as my soul and body and spirit was able to bear. I was all alone, had nobody to tell my troubles to except the Lord. When I got up to speak to the people, and seeing [them] on the fence, on the road, in the grass, my heart seemed to melt within. I throwed myself on the Lord. I saw that night, for the first time, a Mother in the Deity. This was indeed a new scene, a new doctrine for me.[9]

Courage can come from remembering powerful women of the past and by imagining ourselves as part of the future. Imagining ourselves as preachers is coming to terms with our designation as "other." It is imagining a new and inclusive world being drawn out of the old. Just as Rebecca Jackson acknowledged and named her fears, so beginning preachers can be encouraged to name their own experiences of silence and of voice.

- How would you describe your own voice?
- What do you know about the voice of God?
- When has the human voice been a locus of God's presence for you?
- Remember a time when you have been silenced.
- Do you remember a time when shame or fear kept you from speaking? A time when you knew shame and fear because you did not speak?
- Remember a time when you were "voiced."
- Where are the places, sacred spaces in your life, where you can speak freely and honestly?

The struggle for many beginning to preach is to reject controlling images, to envision a new world, and to integrate knowledge deemed personally important. It is helpful to find a safe space for resisting objectification as "other." Nelle Morton in her classic, *The Journey is Home,* describes the women's groups she encountered in her long feminist journey, and rejoices in the gift of women to women in hearing one another into speech. A new kind of seeing and hearing was beginning to be experienced by one group of women after another. Once they recognized in themselves a common oppression, they could hear from one another that which many, more astute and intellectual than they, could not hear. Experiencing grace in this manner has become one of the most powerful liberating forces in the lives of women. Women came to new speech simply because they were being heard.[10]

Finding safe space allows the expression of the "voice" of the authentic self. It allows us to be present to ourselves in such a way that lets us be at peace, reconciled to ourselves, made whole. By asserting our full value as a human being with "voice," we affirm ourselves as good—body, mind, and spirit—

> It's part of the spiritual journey—finding your own voice.
>
> MM

and take our place within the universe as a creation of the Creator. Only when we experience this wholeness within ourselves can we be fully available to commune with and be reconciled to others.

It is not easy to imagine new worlds for ourselves and for others. Our imaginations have been "colonized."[11] Can we imagine a world where women are valued/strong/free? Where women's experience is spoken and heard? Can we imagine a church where women's stories and bodies are part of the sacred tradition?

We open our imaginations to the new, always hoping, of course, to open the imaginations of those in the community so that they, too, can keep dreaming.

The Listening

It was a warm fall afternoon at Memphis Theological Seminary when students gathered in the classroom for a course on "Imagination and Preaching." One of the objectives for the class that day was for students to explore compassion as an imaginative act by becoming aware of the differences in people's views of reality, based on their particular social location. These preachers and "would-be" preachers needed to consider other interpretations of theology and scripture in light of differing cultural contexts.

As Mary Lin prepared imaginary profiles of different conversation partners, she envisioned persons of various nationalities, ages, races, sexes, sexual orientations, abilities, vocations, educational and economic levels, different in terms of their physical and mental health. The selection pool was broad and complex.

You could feel the tension as the class participants reached into a small basket to draw out the profile of a person they might never have encountered. Moans, laughter, and stunned silences filled the room as each student became acquainted with her new worldview. The task before them was difficult, for they were asked to embody the personal profile and imagine themselves as a conversation partner in a small group.

The assignment looked simple. Divide into small groups and discuss the following:

- What is the most pressing issue for people in the world today?
- What is God like for you?
- What do you fear most?
- Read scripture: Luke 6:17–38.
- What is your reaction to this text?
- What is it saying to you?
- What is it saying to the Christian Church today?
- What message does it carry for society in general or for the world?

The conversation was lively as the participants waded into the world of the other, trying to discover the sound of that voice. As people discussed their experience of the process, they confessed that they had been forced to deal with human issues that had never before entered their consciousness. It was impossible for the imagination to grasp fully the experience of the other person, but instead, the exercise readily revealed the prejudices and stereotypes that had shaped the world of the preacher. In the end, many students resolved to listen differently, more carefully and compassionately, to the voices of people unlike themselves.

We are accustomed to thinking about the prophet as the one who speaks. We can think of forceful images, both ancient and contemporary, portraits of women and men who have stood and courageously faced a world in need of the resisting word. We can even quote some of those words—"I have a dream..." "Swords into ploughshares..." "Let justice roll down like water..." "Ain't I a woman?" Strong voices. Memorable voices. These are voices that change and continue to change the world's landscape if we allow it.

But this one who speaks is also called to a vocation of prophetic listening. The prophet listens to God, the source of her life and the giver of "voice." The prophet listens to herself, having come to believe that what she thinks and the way she lives in the world has value, authority. The prophet also listens to the community. She listens to the community because the word is formed there. Word forms community, and community forms word. And she listens, not simply so that her word is relevant and has meaning in its particular context. Her reason for listening is far more important and integral to her calling. She listens because we are people of the incarnation, and we believe that in life experiences God is made manifest. Our experiences are revelatory, and we listen because God is there.

Called back to the covenant and to be in relationship to the speaking and listening God, we move close to the world, so close that we can hear its very weak pulse. As Nelle Morton has said, "If the style of a woman's preaching was not to deliver (to proclaim) the Word but to place her ear close to the pulse of the people, then a new kind of Pentecost would be possible. Each tongue would be loosened and each would be speaking her/his own word and that word would be her/himself."[12]

The preacher realizes that she does not have a singular hold on the truth, recognizes the importance of her relationships with others in the community, recognizes the importance of other distinctive voices in the discernment of truth. Only a "mutual acoustic" can empower all of God's people to discover their voices, to challenge that which silences those on the margins, and to move into a realm of equality that Jesus spoke into each being on earth, the very place where forces (internal and external) limit our freedom to be.[13] Women, with imaginations unleashed and heard into speech, would begin to speak of the realities they know in language that is capable of speaking its truth.

Scott is a minister on staff at my church. He was the first openly gay man to be ordained through this association. It was one hard struggle to get that through. It will be interesting to see how his voice emerges as a gay man in a mainstream denomination. Scott knows the gay community. He listens to that voice. When you know your own people and your own experience, then you struggle with how you speak to that community, and how you bring that community's experience to a tradition in such a way that it will speak to all. It is a fascinating process to watch, because it relates so much to what women or African Americans have gone through. Anyone who speaks without having listened doesn't have much to say.

CC

Dietrich Bonhoeffer has said: "Images are not lies, they point to reality and let the reality appear through them. Images differ; those of a child's are not an adult's, and those of an inhabitant of the desert are different from the city dweller's. Nevertheless they remain true, just as human speech and ideas remain true, to the extent that God remains in them."[14]

Thus, preaching requires that the self be engaged, fully engaged in the task; the perspectives of one who dwells in the desert are not the same as the one who dwells in the city. Learning to listen to the self is an important component of the hermeneutical and exegetical tasks. Patricia Hill Collins demonstrates how women may use many different strategies in their quest for the independent voice, in their quest for inspiration of God's spirit. In Alice Walker's *The Color Purple,* Celie writes herself free. The listening God hears her into speech when no one else will. Eventually, having broken her silence with the written word, she is able to dialogue with others. Janie, in *Their Eyes Were Watching God,* tells her story to a good friend, talking herself free. In Ntozake Shange's *For Colored Girls,* the women gather around the one who shares her life's pain. They listen until she says, "I found God in myself and loved her fiercely."

Spiritual practices result in a sense of the innerness of self, which helps the marginalized confront injustices of the status quo. Spiritual practices move a person toward a link or web with all creation.

Our experience of contemporary culture raises questions about our ability to discover that authentic voice that we want and need to hear. With our world constantly bombarded by voices, how can we expect to discover our own "voice"? Do we really have the ability to "voice" an authentic self, or are we simply echoes of the competing voices around us? What does God have to do with finding one's voice? How does God participate in the process in which the preacher recognizes the evil of domination to silence and then gathers the strength to speak? Can the preacher know when her voice has been "found"? Can the community?

Like a wooden mannequin propped on the knee of a ventriloquist, we often find words passing through our lips that sound foreign and strange, as if they are coming from something outside of us. Too frequently we allow ourselves to become "conduits" for the cultural voices around us. Is it possible for us to bracket the cacophony of competing voices in order to explore the silence of our own interiority long enough to hear our own authentic "voice" trying to find expression within us? Yes. Finding a voice of our own is an essential part of our salvation.

By finding our voice we affirm ourselves as good—body, mind, and spirit—and take our place within the universe as a creation of the Creator.

According to Patricia Hill Collins, black women intellectuals have long explored an internal, private space of consciousness that enables them to cope with, and perhaps eventually transcend, the confines of classism, sexism and racism.[15]

Women must listen carefully so that, somewhere in their recesses, they will discover an internal system of authority that will allow them to take their places alongside external authority systems that have attempted to define them.[16]

John McClure, thinking about seminary students who are now being prepared for pastoral ministry, says that preachers coming out of seminaries are aware that social location and varying exegetical methodologies have influence on their biblical interpretations. They see that their own presuppositions produce meaning. They understand the biblical text as more than a literary-historical artifact or object of devotion. Because of this, he reasons that seminary students will be more open to acknowledging the limitations of their own reading and more willing to explore interpretations that come from other social locations and traditions. This is no doubt true. It is also true, however, that many who are preparing to preach in the face of strong and unrelenting resistance need to be reminded that their own perspective is of value and that they are important members of the hermeneutical conversation.[17]

The prophetic preacher will be one who listens carefully to the biblical text from which she preaches. It is important to bring heart, listening ear, and mind to the task. Communities deserve and desire to know about the intricacies, the difficulties, and the tensions within the text. They live with unanswered questions, doubts about all that they have learned. Bringing a good and credible interpretation to the community is one way of "awakening voice" within the congregation. Hearing the preacher voice her own questions will invite and perhaps persuade them to ask theirs.

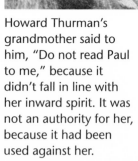

Howard Thurman's grandmother said to him, "Do not read Paul to me," because it didn't fall in line with her inward spirit. It was not an authority for her, because it had been used against her.

RN

We are heirs of a great legacy. Generations of biblical scholars have now studied, analyzed, and brought systems and categories of thought to bear upon the biblical text. From their historical roots many "criticisms" have grown, bringing to us as students of the biblical text a depth and breadth of information related to the text's history, form, rhetoric, structure, and tendencies. These scholars have come to the text with their imaginations. They have listened, and they have named what has been seen. As preachers (not as substitute for our own imaginings but in concert with them), we can listen to those insights that have been generated as potential correctives or enhancements of our own. Read. And read with suspicion. For as surely as the biblical text reflects a patriarchal bias, so does much of the scholarship about it. Do not be deceived.

The metaphor of voice implies that the use of all of self is engaged in creating a sermon. It involves a vigorous and active use of the mind that can ask penetrating questions. Wisdom prompts us to seek knowledge.

The Naming

Mary Donovan Turner and Joe Driskill were teaching a class together on Protestant Spirituality and Preaching at PSR. Throughout the experience, Joe taught Mary about the many time-honored exercises that have been a part of her tradition for centuries, exercises that bring woman and man to a prayerful encounter with the biblical text. She describes her experience in this way:

> On one Monday afternoon, we introduced a group of 80 people to an exercise called "Luther's Four-Stranded Garland." It is a way of prayer. Legend has it that one afternoon Martin Luther's barber asked him how to pray. And in response, Luther outlined for him this process of listening to the text, individually or communally, and listening for what God might be saying through it. The parable chosen for the exercise was a short one, one replete with challenges, struggles, difficulties, but one which may also be rendering to us a word of grace. We then engaged the class in this process:

> 1. Select a scripture passage or other devotional reading to which you would like to direct your attention. You may wish to follow the Lectionary readings. We did. We read Luke 13:6–9.

> And he told this parable: "A man had a fig tree planted in his vineyard, and he came seeking fruit on it and found none. And he said to the vinedresser, 'Lo these three years I have come seeking fruit on this fig tree, and I find none. Cut it down; why should it use up the ground?' And he answered him, 'Let it alone, sir, this year also, till I dig about it and put on manure. And if it bears fruit next year, well and good; but if not, you can cut it down.'"

2. Sit quietly and take a few moments to slow down. Get in touch with what you are feeling at the present moment. Prepare yourselves for prayer in the manner you find most helpful.

3. First reading of the text: Listen quietly as it is being read.

4. Second reading: Read more slowly and listen for the instruction that you hear in the text. This may come from a word, phrase, or image; it may come from the sense of the whole passage. If you feel comfortable sharing quietly, say the word, phrase, or image that "stands out" for you.

5. Third reading: As you hear the text, listen for something for which you would like to give thanks. Allow the sense of thanksgiving to fill your presence. Notice your own affect as you hear the text.

6. Fourth reading: As you hear this reading of the scripture, allow yourself to confess your own sinfulness. Be aware of how you have "missed the mark" in your own life. Be aware of the affective dimension of this experience.

7. Fifth reading: As you hear this last reading, contemplate the way God is present to you in the word, phrase, image, or feeling that stands out for you. Rest in this feeling and let it lead you to resting in God. If you are comfortable, share something of this experience with others.

8. Close with a personal prayer of thanksgiving.[18]

> It is not surprising that the conversations in the smaller groups were able to generate conversation about some of the difficulties of this short parable. Some, for instance, named the owner's readiness (even after three years) to cut down the fig tree because it did not yet bear fruit. Some named their gratitude and thanksgiving for times in their lives when they felt they were given a second chance. But it was in response to step six—allow yourself to confess your own sinfulness—that the discussion about the parable was most interesting. Participants named the ways they were "impatient," the ways they labeled others by their own standards of productiveness or lack of it, ways they were impatient with themselves. This exercise became an exercise in "naming" the ways we are in the world. The naming led to confession.

When Mary does this exercise, as she has done over the course of several years, now with every text on which she preaches, she has found that an additional "step" is helpful for her. She adds: Is there anything in this text that makes me afraid? In this text she realized, for instance, that she lived with the fear sometimes that she was not "productive" enough—that she was simply using up the ground. She looks for fear in texts, because fear is considered a constant companion. A student told her after doing this exercise that he would add: Is there anything in the text that makes me angry? He said that just as fear was a constant companion, anger was also.

This method, as well as other spiritual practices, can allow the listening process to focus itself into an act of naming. Prophetic preaching involves naming the old worlds out of which we would like to move. Some of us would like to move out of the world of fear. The lamenters in the psalms often wanted to move out of the world governed by their "enemies," and into a world of health, safety, and refuge. In the penitential psalms they named their sin and their hope so that they would be drawn into a new world of forgiveness and peace.

We are not to stop here, of course, with the naming of our private indiscretions and longings. Prophetic preaching requires that we name the injustices in the world. All the forces that alienate and silence, all the forces that keep women and men, who are created in the sound of God, from speaking their truths in a world that desperately needs to hear them, must be exposed. We must address systemic evil, the oppressive systems that unrelentingly muffle the sound of some, showing preference and priority for others. Every wrong needs a voice.

"Feminist preaching as a ministry of resistance understands the magnitude of human oppression and injustice in the world and seeks to address it. The evil produced by interlocking systems of oppression and the injustice sustained by acts of individual and collective violence give rise to an urgent and distinctive homiletic. The methodologies and theological convictions that inform this understanding of preaching are utterly rooted in the commitments of liberation theology. Liberation theologians seek to shape theology and the practice of ministry in response to the concrete realities of human suffering and oppression, toward a vision of liberation and restoration. The primary and ultimate agenda of resistance and liberation forms the ground out of which a ministry of resistance emerges."[19]

Prophetic preaching ultimately involves carefully analyzing one's own preaching for any

Many times we, as women, could have spoken out about issues, and we remained silent, even though we knew God had given us the authority to speak out. When we don't speak out, we become those who silence other voices. *SLK* oppressive tendencies. An example of when preaching stifles voice, rather than awakens it, comes from Thomas Troeger's *The Parable of The Ten Preachers*.[20] In the story, Marjorie, a member of the class, is talking about the most memorable sermon she has ever heard.

Marjorie was a nurse, and she recounts to her preaching class a Tuesday night when she was working in the emergency room. She describes the children brought in with high temperature, and the crowded condition of the waiting room; it was difficult to meet the needs of all who needed care.

Things were just beginning to come under control, when a man came through the door and walked up to the desk. His arm was around a woman's shoulder; he was holding her up. She huddled inside an overcoat, collar upturned. Her small eyes were looking out, one puffy and dark. The man started talking, insisting on seeing a doctor right away. "My wife here fell down the stoop. Slipped on the ice. We came home, and well, we'd both had a little too much, and I said, 'Honey, watch the top step,' her being in heels and everything. Then down she goes, landing on her cheek on those sharp steps." Marjorie knew these were members of her church. She knew they had been to the emergency room before. The woman turned down any offers for help, for safe shelter.

That next Sunday, the man and woman were in church. Marjorie watched them and listened to the hymns that the community sang and the prayers that were offered, in light of the battered woman huddled on the back pew. The prayer? "Almighty Father, we have sinned against you, by claiming more than is ours." Marjorie said to the class, "These were not the words she needed to pray. She had not claimed too much for herself. She needed to claim more." And the sermon? It was from Second Corinthians. Since God did not count our trespasses against us, we must not count our trespasses against each other. The preacher painted visions of what might happen if wives and husbands, neighbors and nations would only forgive each other. The preacher was speaking words from the clouds, straight from heaven to earth, as if they were universally true, when they were not.

Marjorie was describing a sermon, a prayer, a service of worship that stifled that woman's expression, that kept her from realizing her potential as a voiced creature, formed and fashioned in the sound of God. They kept her from crying out to God in lament; she did not know that God would listen to her pain.

Prophetic preaching involves naming the oppressive and patriarchal nature of the biblical text. The preacher is empowered by the Spirit to take back the scriptures, listening and speaking of them painfully, angrily, prophetically, hopefully, lovingly, and gracefully.[21] A woman must read the biblical text both with an eye toward the invisibility of women and the expressions of violence against them, along with the accountings of women's leadership and witness.[22] A woman must read with suspicion, asking questions about how the cultural and ecclesial motives render a particular telling of a story. Fine feminist scholars such as Rosemary Radford Ruether, Elisabeth Schüssler Fiorenza, Mary Daly, Marjorie Procter-Smith, Mary Ann Tolbert (and a host of others) have defined and described for us this relationship with the biblical text. Can the text be redeemed? Is there, buried beneath the layers of our text, a liberating word for women? Wrestling with the text through a variety of perspectives and strategies leads these scholars to make radically different decisions about church affiliation and scriptural authority. They are clear, each of them, however, that the patriarchal and androcentric nature of the biblical text must be named. It has served the interests of men. Moreover, traditional texts, models of interpretations, and lectionaries all must be examined in light of women's experience. Through this exploration, new thoughts are generated, new questions are raised, and new sermons will be preached.

There isn't a person on the religious right who doesn't use scripture to oppress. *AS*

Hope is lodged in the naming. It is only when the oppression, the suffering, and the pain of the world continue to be named and proclaimed that we can continue to hope. William Sloane Coffin has said, "Hope resists, hopelessness adapts."[23] The expression of hope from the preacher must be as strong and as clear as the naming of the despair. We must ask ourselves, "Do we believe that injustice can be eradicated? Can we even imagine a time when the weeping will end?"

Women seem to feel a more internal spiritual calling to ministry, and that often gets lost in traditionally male pulpits. You don't want to be talking about your personal experience in the pulpit because it isn't academic enough, it isn't objective enough, or there hasn't been adequate theological discourse among German theologians about it. So I think that's part of the frozenness I feel when talking about personal experience from the pulpit. *CC*

Imagining. Listening. Naming. These are all done with and by the preacher who has come to trust her own ability to do all of these things, inspired and fed by the listening/speaking God who has called her. Her self is engaged mightily in the task, because preaching demands it of her. The "word" yearns to find its way to community through her distinctive, authentic, authoritative, resistant and relational voice that makes it ever new.

Beginning with the call of Moses, biblical narrative highlights the role of the prophet and prophetic speech as central to the relationship between God and humanity. Continuing at the baptism of Jesus and the experience of Pentecost, prophetic speech is the agency of God. The prophet is a listener, a person with supersensitivity to the voice that is beyond the cacophony of voices. The prophet is a person who has the power to imagine worlds that are not yet seen or heard. The power to speak and name comes as gift and terror through the presence of the Spirit in and through the person of the prophet. Hope-filled preaching creates within the imaginations of women a vision of their giftedness and ability; claims their right to speak; encourages them to listen to the world, God, and self so that an authentic world emerges; empowers them to name the injustices of the world so that newness can be drawn forth. This is where hope is found.

And we must keep on preaching the prophetic message. In Luke, women are called to proclaim what they have seen so that the world will know about the tomb that is empty. It is as if the resurrection is rendered powerless without the human voice to proclaim it. Your voice? Ours?

Echoes

What is the journey like—the journey from silence to voice? Is it not the movement from the emptiness of despair to the fullness of our exuberance? Is this movement not a continuous revolution? It happens not once, not twice, but over and over again, always moving in faith toward a new future, a new heaven and a new earth. For this reason, the journey itself is the task of theology.

The theological question persists: what in the world is God doing in our experience? This is a question that suggests that God is on the move—initiating new speech, calling us to new action, new relationships. God calls us to listen to the world, to our own hearts and minds, to God. God calls us to name what we see and imagine what cannot yet be seen. This is frightening because it is a call to embrace the unfamiliar and the untried, to risk! Would it not be safer to stay on familiar ground and remain silent? Would it not be safer to stay with what we know, the true and tried, the fossilized, the static beliefs, the fixed theological formulations, all the old answers to the old questions, the frozen canon, the bland certainty? No. It is illusion to think that living in silence, unwilling to name the old and imagine the new, is to live in safety.

This world continues to enshrine the monological, exclusive discourse called patriarchy. It is a confusing maze and, perhaps, a closed circle of certainty. There, God's call to women (a call to dialogue and inclusiveness) cannot be tolerated. It is, however, the only call that can bring salvation or wholeness, because it is an inclusive word.

Who can speak the prophetic and inclusive word in a world of enshrined certainty? Only God's agent can do that work. Still, it is hard, perhaps impossible, because the ones who can speak feel woefully inadequate. Ah, here is the bind: the only ones who can authentically speak the liberating word are the prisoners who feel powerless to speak. They have been reduced to silence—full of sadness, suffering, betrayal, doubt, grief, loss, disappointment, hurt, and anger. These are the experiences that confirm them in the old world that is already passing away!

God is doing something new in women's experience. Can't you perceive it? Can't you hear it? Can't you feel it? God, the faithful God, is drawing something glorious out of the old in words that resonate with Mary's: "My soul magnifies the Lord, and my spirit rejoices in God my Savior" (Luke 1:46–47).

Yes, the journey is from the emptiness of despair to the fullness of our exuberance. This requires struggle against the old and enslaving powers, a rejection of controlling images, and a daring willingness to go forth into a future that has not yet been named, because it is a future that makes all things new. It is a continuous revolution and evolution. Can you perceive it?

Chapter 8

Imagining, Listening, Naming: Three Sermons

I Dream a World

Texts: Isaiah 11:1–9, Romans 8:18–25, Hebrews 11:1–3, 8–16; 12:1–2

A few years ago, an exhibit came to the Brooks Museum of Art in Overton Park. The title of the exhibit was "I Dream A World." Around the walls of the gallery hung photographs of seventy-five African American women who had made a difference in the world because of their dreams. Life-sized portraits of famous women like Coretta Scott King, Oprah Winfrey, Leontyne Price, Merlie Evers, and Odetta hung side by side with the faces of virtual unknowns:

- *Septima Poinsette Clark*—one of the most effective, and yet unsung heroes of the civil rights movement, who believed that literacy was the key to empowerment. Working with Highlander Folk School and the Southern Christian Leadership Conference in Georgia, she developed innovative citizenship schools throughout the south.
- *Josephine Riley Matthews*—a licensed midwife who safely delivered more than 1,300 babies, black and white, in rural South Carolina. She said, "I'll bet you one thing, if the man had to have the first baby there wouldn't be but two in the family. Yes sir, let him have the first one and the woman the next one, and his time wouldn't come around no more." She graduated from high school

at age 74 and was named the state's Woman of the Year and Outstanding Older American.

• *Marva Nettles Collins*—founded Westside Preparatory School in Chicago in 1975 to educate the young children of Chicago's mean streets. "This school is all about service," she says. "Every child has to tutor five other children in their neighborhood. It's part of our motto: Entrance to learn, exit to serve." Using pension funds from fourteen years of teaching in public schools, she built a schoolroom in her home. That school, which now occupies two buildings, has grown from 18 to 250 students. "I think it is very interesting that teachers from monied systems all over the world come into this very spartan facility to learn our methodology. I cannot change the world, but I do not have to conform to it."

The gallery was filled with the portraits of women who dared to dream a world, and lived those dreams into realities through their courage and love. As the poet Maya Angelou described them:

> They are not apparitions; they are not superwomen. Despite their majestic struggle they are not larger than life. Their humanness is evident in their accessibility. We are able to enter their photographs and enter into the spirit of these women and rejoice in their courage and nearness. Precious jewels all. Thanks to their persistence, art, sublime laughter and love we may all yet survive our grotesque history.

In another gallery, the gallery of our imaginations, hang other portraits of prophets, apostles, saints. The inscription under each portrait reads, "Dreamer of Worlds." The prophet Isaiah proclaimed a vision of the world shaped by the righteousness of a promised Messiah, whose justice pronounces the fullness of God's glory. A world of peace: calf and bear, leopard and lamb, child, and snake. Playing and dining together in harmony. "A dream of shalom."

The apostle Paul envisioned a world of bodies and rivers and mountains and voices all restored to perfect wholeness by the power of God's redemption. Because of the grace revealed in Christ's death and resurrection, a new world was in view. The Spirit gave the power to women and men to see visions and dream dreams.

Joining the portraits of Isaiah and Paul are the figures throughout time who, through faith, lived into their vision of God's promised world of peace. Mothers and fathers, preachers and teachers, servants and martyrs all line the walls of the tradition to encourage us to move ahead. Through the communion of saints we are able to enter into their presence and find encouragement and nearness from their spirits for our journey.

In the mid-sixties during the March on Washington, Dr. Martin Luther King, Jr., delivered his great speech "I Have a Dream." This dream led him down streets, across bridges, into lonely jail cells, and eventually to Memphis, Tennessee. The night before his assassination, he spoke at the Mason Temple Church of God in Christ. "I don't know what will happen," he prophesied. "Got some troubles ahead. Doesn't matter to me now. For I've been to the mountaintop. I don't mind. Like anybody I'd like to live a long life; longevity has its place. I'm not concerned about that. I just want to do God's will. God has allowed me to go up to the mountain, and I've looked over and I've seen the promised land. I may not yet be there with you, but I want you to know tonight that we as a people will get to the promised land. So I'm happy tonight. I'm not worried about anything. I'm not fearing any man. Mine eyes have seen the glory of the coming of the Lord"[1] (April 4, 1968).

What about you? Have your eyes beheld the glory of the coming of the Lord? What do you dream of? What vision keeps you moving ahead, struggling and singing, suffering and shouting? What longing sings out from the depth of your soul? As we come together in Christ's name, what kind of world do we long for?

I invite you to speak your dream aloud together right now and paint a picture of the world of our dreams. Call out your dream so that we can see it together. Begin your statement with the phrase, "I long for a world where..." And those who wish to affirm that dream may respond with "Amen."

(Time is given for the congregation to express their longings and visions.)

Hold fast to your visions. Keep on dreaming dreams. Let us move ahead into new creation and live toward the coming day of God's glorious peace.

Mary Lin Hudson
Memphis Theological Seminary Chapel

About the sermon:

As I prepared this sermon for the MTS community, I reflected on the power of prophetic imagination to lead communities out of the old and into the new. The prophetic vision that is described in the biblical texts presents a compelling ideal, bringing hope to the people of faith. At the same time, it serves as an act of resistance, refusing to allow the present order to define the life of humanity. The same Spirit that inspired this vision continues to inspire the people of God today.

Instead of talking about prophetic vision, or explaining the purpose of these realities, I wanted the sermon to move people to listen to the prophetic voice within them and to find courage to express their ideas aloud. For that reason, I provided a moment toward the end of the sermon where the conversation shifted from the preacher to the congregation. The expression of visions was not just an imaginative act; it empowered the community to claim the new for themselves.

Too often sermons appeal to "bigger than life" persons as the heroes of the faith. In this sermon, I chose relatively unknown people whose lives had made a significant difference in their world. I hoped that the listener would recognize the power of someone who was like them. By concentrating on African American women, I chose to offer an example of persons who, as a group, have been systematically silenced through the years. Yet each of these women demonstrated strength, wisdom, and compassion that moved them beyond the limitations imposed by the outside world.

The words of Dr. Martin Luther King, Jr., have inspired millions of people throughout the world. The members of the Memphis community, however, are forever haunted by the memory and the shame of his assassination that took place in their midst. Repeating the words of his speech the night before he died provides more than an imaginative act for this particular congregation. It is a remembering of the tension of that historic moment and the prophetic accuracy of his words. These particular words of the sermon were not just profound for the listeners; they were electric.

Without the imaginative act that leads us to listen to the voice within, people would remain captive to the limitations of the world around them. That is why preaching and imagination go hand in hand. When preaching leads to the community's expression of vision and hope, it has announced good news. People are being set free.

Staying Power

Text: John 20:1–18

I have spent most of my life on the periphery of things. I often find myself waiting for the right time, the right moment to enter into all that is happening around me. I miss some opportunities that way. By the time I'm ready to speak, often the conversation has passed me by. Then it's just too late.

But over the years there have been some really wonderful advantages to being an introvert. It has allowed me to become an observer of life. To watch the interplay and communication patterns of those around me; their participation and posture during conversations has been fascinating. I have developed this power of observation to a fine art. At committee meetings, faculty meetings, planning sessions, retreats, I watch and I watch and I listen and I listen to what is going on around me.

I also watch and listen when I read a really good story. I can conjure up those characters in my mind almost as convincingly as if they were really standing right there in front of me. I notice how they move. I hear them speak. I study them as they engage each other, ignore each other, try to outdo each other, support each other, comfort each other.

As I sat down and read John's story about Mary Magdalene, I did just that. I sat back and I watched and I listened...

I found myself alone, sitting in the midst of the graves of people I did not know. It was dark; I do remember that. Very dark. I couldn't see, but who would have thought there would be anything to see? There was.

Suddenly she was standing right in front of me. And then, just as suddenly as she had appeared, she disappeared back into the night. Frightened. Alone. I could understand her leaving so quickly; it was a frightening place to be, standing there in front of the tomb with that stone rolled away. She left, more quickly than she had come, and again the night air, the darkness, was silent. As silent as death.

I wondered if I should stay, if this was all there was to the story, but before I could go I heard footsteps again—someone, no two, running down the path. As they got closer and I could see them, I could tell it wasn't the woman who had returned; it was two men. Running together. One was faster than the other, and when he got to the tomb, he stopped. He bent down and looked in. I couldn't tell what he saw in there, but it was enough to convince him that life was better outside the tomb.

And then the other, the one who couldn't run quite as fast as the first, ran right into the tomb. Didn't take the time to stop, to look, to crouch, just ran down the path and into the tomb. Convinced that it was safe, the other went in also, saw what there was to see, I suppose, and then they left together side by side.

I had been watching them so intently, I hadn't noticed that she had returned. I was glad, really. She had come to the tomb and left so quickly I felt as if I hadn't had the time to get to know her. I wanted to. Now she was there again; she was weeping. I suspected that someone really important to her had died. Must have been a parent, friend, spouse, a child. I wanted to know. And as she stood there, consciously or unconsciously, I didn't know for sure, she inched her way to that opening. Ever so slowly, very slowly, she inched toward that opening.

I had hoped that she would leave, actually; the pain of being there seemed so great. But she stayed. And she stayed. And she stayed. I wanted her to go away or at least to turn her eyes, thinking that if she would, the pain would be lessened and the tears would stop falling. I wanted to go and comfort her myself. But I just watched helplessly in the darkness as she stayed, and stayed, and stayed. She moved slowly, very slowly toward the tomb's entrance.

Then I heard the voices, could have been one, but it sounded like more, and they were asking her my question! The very same question that had been burning inside me. They asked her:

"Woman, why are you weeping?"

Finally she spoke. I heard her voice, a faint voice, cracking with disappointment and grief. "They have taken him away. I don't know where they've taken him." Then I understood. She had lost this person twice—whoever he was—she had lost him when he died. Now she had lost him again. I could understand this kind of grief.

We were not alone in the garden. Another voice out of the darkness:

"Woman, why are you weeping?"

I thought for a moment someone was talking to me, but no, he was talking to her. And suddenly her voice came, stronger now, desperate, pleading, loud enough to wake up the world from its sleep. "If you know where they have put him, tell me where he is. I will pick him up and carry him away."

And then...he called her by name. She turned and said softly, "Teacher." He told her to go, to tell the others that she had seen him and something about this God they shared. Finally she left; I could understand why she didn't want to go. Perhaps she was afraid of losing him a third time. What if she never saw him again? But she left, and the teacher left. I was alone, again, in the darkness.

I wished I had talked with this woman. Like so many times in my life, I let the opportunity escape me. Quickly it comes, and then it is gone. But as I sat there, and as daylight began to fill the sky, I realized I didn't need to talk to her at all. Just by my watching her, she had surely become my teacher, just as the one who had died had been hers. I almost felt as if this grand drama had been played our right before my eyes so that I could learn something, so that we could learn something about death and life and grief and persistence. It was as if this story played out in front of me was a grand invitation, an invitation to you and to me and to the church who preserved this story for us. An invitation to go to those places in the world where there seems to be no hope—only death and despair. An invitation to go straight to the tomb and stay there. Plant ourselves firmly there, and even if the realities are too painful, **not** to avert our eyes, **not** to close our ears, and **not** to move away! Just stay there in the darkness, shivering from the cold, but standing there with whoever is there. Weeping for them, with them. But never, ever running away. Just standing there until the world who is watching cries out:

"People, why are you weeping?"

Then we would take the world by the hand and lead the world to the entrance, and we would say, "Look into the tomb." We would show them who is living there. We would show them that small child with his mother and father huddled together. They are afraid. They told their child that they were coming to a new country, a country that would be their home, their safe home. And we would hear that small child whispering:

"No hay vida aqui. No hay vida aqui."

"There is no life here."

And in the corner?

There is a woman there, a vacant look in her eyes. She knows only about a love that is cruel and abusive.

There is a child with parched, cracking lips and swollen stomach, dying from hunger.

There is a person dying alone from a disease that sadly yet has no cure.

They are all there; they have given up any hope for life. We would want to turn away.

But Mary says to us, "Stay there. Stay and stay and stay. Just stay, until in the midst of the noisy silence of the darkness...an alleluia is heard, maybe faint at first, but an alleluia...maybe cold and broken, but an alleluia, a song of survival, a note of hopefulness that in the middle of the grief life brings pouring upon us, somebody is there, and somebody will stay there, stay right there until tears of sadness become tears of joy because then we all know that God is there with us.

That's what I learned from that woman who stood there at the entrance of the tomb that night. I learned that for the world to come to know something about God's presence we must keep our tear stained faces gazing toward all that is seemingly dead and dying until...until the world hears that melody.

Alleluia....

Mary Donovan Turner
Preached in the Chapel of the Great Commission
Pacific School of Religion

About the sermon:

In April 1996, I was asked to preach the Easter sermon during the regular chapel service at Pacific School of Religion. As was the custom at the time, each week a faculty member would work with a small group of students to plan the week's service. In this case, I worked with three women for several weeks. We chose to use the gospel text John 20:1–18.

When we first sat down together, we felt as if we were joining a conversation that had been going on for centuries. We listened to the narrative and began to share with one another memories associated with it. I learned a great deal about these students that I had not known, even though two were my advisees. Such is the nature of planning worship together. The stories they told were sad, funny, challenging; a sense of community began to build as we found ourselves standing with Mary at the tomb of Jesus. We explored every word of the story, thought about it, felt with it, and prayed over it.

Two weeks later we began to read what others had written about it. We chose commentaries and eventually several lectionary journals. One in particular had a marked influence on the direction of both sermon and liturgy. The words in the journal went something like this: "Mary demonstrates great emotion at the tomb. It is her inability to overcome her grief that causes her to linger there. This kind of emotional display renders women incapable of leadership; it impedes their ability to be strong and worthy disciples." I suspect you can begin to imagine the response that the four seminary women had to those words! There was an emphatic naming of the commentator's stereotypes and prejudices! As appalling as these words were, when read with "suspicion," they brought clarity to our own work. We began to focus on the value of Mary's expression of grief, her willingness to stay at the tomb, her "staying power." As is often the case, it was in reading something with which we disagreed that we found our own thinking. We wanted to affirm women who throughout history have often cared for the sick and the dying and have been found lamenting as the funeral procession passed.

What issues/concerns were on our minds those weeks? We were aware of a pervasive discussion in our own state about severely limiting health and educational benefits for children of immigrants. We had experienced the death of a student with AIDS. You will find these children and our beloved friend, along with others we knew in our ministries, huddled together in the tomb of Jesus.

The service began with a dramatic rendering of the gospel text. The first sounds heard in the chapel that morning were those of Mary—a rich, profound, bone-chilling sound of weeping and wailing. After the sermon there was silence, broken by a single voice singing softly an "alleluia." Others joined slowly until every person in the community was singing with great exuberance and passion an affirmation of the possibility of hope that can grow out of despair.[2]

The Jonah Complex
Text: Jonah 1:1–3

Let me tell you about a moment that changed my life. It was the spring of my freshman year of college. I was a student at the University of Nebraska, with a major in piano and a minor in violin. I was walking across the campus one day, and as I passed the Business Administration Building, I had a call. As clear as a bell, a voice inside me said, "You need to leave this place, move on, as soon as you can. If you don't leave now, you never will, and this isn't where you're supposed to be." I spent the next months researching schools, talking to people, getting applications in. Within a year, I was studying philosophy in Williamstown, Massachusetts. When people asked me why I made the sudden transition, I just said something like, "It seemed like it was time to move on."

But it was more than that. To this day, I know that what I heard that day as I walked across the University of Nebraska campus was a calling, and I knew if I didn't listen to it, I wouldn't be living the life that I was supposed to be living.

Virtually every religious tradition—Judaism, Christianity, Buddhism, Shamanism—involves a ritual of "call" or "being called." Hindus build in a sense of "call" in the greeting "Namaste," which means, "I welcome the person that I see, and I also welcome and greet the soul within you." By saying "Namaste," they "call forth" that sacred identity in each one of us.

Most often, Christian worship begins with a kind of "call"—a distinct sound, a summons, that allows us to move from one way of thinking to another. Pilgrims in the seventeenth century drummed as a way of calling worshipers out of the routine of the day into an attitude of worship. Here at First Congregational, we begin each worship service with a proclamation, a "Call to Worship."

Whether they exist as established parts of our religious rituals, or whether they come to us in special moments, the purpose of calls is to open us, to awaken us to the voice of God and to the murmurings of our own souls. A popular book has the title *Wake Up Calls*. Calls are an invitation to awaken, to reconnect, to discern what we've not been recognizing, to pay attention in new ways. Calls move us out of the ordinary routines we've established into a state of awareness where we are ready for something new to enter. They invite us to connect with ourselves and to connect with the voice of the sacred.

A call summons us to listen. Living means being called, being spoken to. Our spiritual growth has a great deal to do with listening to the voice of God as it speaks to us, dialoguing with the God who speaks to us, actualizing the truth spoken within our spirits at these moments of dialogue.

You know, the word "religion" actually comes from the Latin word *religare*, which means "reconnect." Religion means, in other words, to "reconnect," to find something that we already have, to remember something that we already know. To be called is to remember ourselves, re-attach what has become forgotten, severed, lost along the way.

James Hillman put it this way. "You are born," he said, "with a character. It is given as a gift, as the old stories say, from the guardians upon your birth...Each person enters the world called. The difficulty is re-connecting, re-membering what we already, at some point, know—finding what we've always had."

An absolutely critical part of our spiritual lives has to do with re-membering—remembering the character we were born with, vocations, our callings. They may be calls to do something—to start that business, to begin painting, to divorce, to move to a new city. They may be calls to be something—to be more patient, less fearful, more assertive, less manipulative. They may be dramatic. They may be hard to detect. Some of us have clear calls—decisive moments when we realize something, commit to something, see the direction our life needs to take.

But most of us don't. Most of the time, our calls don't come directly. They come in nudges, intuitions, and hints. They come as a whisper, not a thundering chorus. The story of Elijah speaks of a "still, small voice." Calls come hesitantly, with pauses. If we aren't listening carefully, we miss them. And even if we hear them, they are easy to ignore. The channels through which we hear our calls are like pierced ears—we have to keep the earring in, or they close up. Most of us won't experience the call of God as a voice that thunders from the sky. It will come quietly as we keep channels open and allow ourselves to gradually hear the murmurs beneath the surface noise.

Listening to the "still, small voice" is never easy. There are many obstacles that keep us from hearing, keep us from re-membering. Today, I'd like to focus on one of those obstacles. It's what psychologist Abraham Maslow called "The Jonah Complex." I think a lot of us suffer from it. What is it? Maslow described it as "the fear of one's own greatness" or "running away from one's own best talents."[3]

The Jonah Complex has to do with avoiding the agenda that God has for our lives, keeping the stakes low, limiting the terrain and the impact. The phrase comes from one of the most popular stories in the Bible—the story of Jonah.

You know how it goes. God called Jonah to preach to the people of Nineveh, and Jonah didn't want to go. He didn't want to go because he didn't feel up to the challenge. He didn't trust his preaching, didn't trust his pastoral skills, didn't trust that he would be able to handle what he was attempting to do. And he didn't want to go to Nineveh. If he was going to stick his neck out for anybody, it wasn't going to be them.

So, rather than going to Nineveh, he takes off in the other direction, to Tarshish. Geographically, this is the equivalent of heading to San Diego rather than Bar Harbor—as far in the other direction as you can go. But you won't be surprised to learn that Jonah couldn't trick God. God offered Jonah a "wake-up call" in the form of a brutal and violent storm. The sailors struggled to keep the boat afloat. What they didn't realize was that one man had all the power to subdue the storm. Jonah could still the sea, save himself, and save all of them by acknowledging his part in creating it.

What is Jonah doing instead? Sleeping! Jonah was in a state of denial—not acting on what he knew, not taking responsibility for the mess he was creating. The captain of the ship served as his "spirit of wakefulness" by confronting him with his responsibility for the impending disaster. And Jonah finally 'fessed up. He told the crew members to throw him overboard. When they did, Jonah was swallowed by a large fish and lived there for three days until he was spit out on the shores of Nineveh, a new man.

In that belly of the fish, Jonah learned that he couldn't run from his call, even though it was bigger than he wanted his life to be. Jonah's sin was that he wanted less for himself than God wanted for him. He had no desire to find the limelight, to enter a controversy, to move center stage and become part of a larger drama.

And can't we sympathize? I taught a class last year where I asked college-age students to imagine what their futures would look like—what the future held for them. One student wrote that he thought he'd die in a car accident in a year or so. Concerned for his emotional and spiritual health, I set up an appointment to talk with him. To my surprise, he wasn't depressed or anxious about his future. He just wanted to get out of the assignment as easily as possible. If he died in a year, there wasn't much to write. He cut his story short. It was easier that way.

Jonah wanted to do the same thing. He wanted to keep the script simple, contained, easy. It's an all-too-human thing to do. None of us really wants to be a prophet, a pioneer, an artist. We hear our calling and we realize it will demand more than we want to give. So we distract ourselves by counting our blessings, by redecorating our houses, by planning that vacation.

We suffer from the Jonah Complex. No one wants a life tipped upside down. It's easier to sleep in the bottom of the boat and pretend that everything's all right rather than enter that ocean of chaos and change. But any creative endeavor, any calling worth having, forces us to enter that ocean of chaos—the world of formlessness and potential.

A calling demands everything we have to give. It asks what we'll put on the line, how much we're willing to risk. It's the classic spiritual paradox. We have to be willing to die before we'll really find life. We have to give up security, comfort, and familiarity before we gain the new life that a call invites. We have to trust in what we can become, invest in what we can become, work toward our own evolution. Jesus challenged us and encouraged us along this risky path all the time. Remember the Gospel of John where Jesus said, "I tell you, the one who believes in me will also do the works that I do and, in fact, will do greater works than these, because I am going to God. I will do whatever you ask in my name."

I think that the church suffers from a Jonah Complex, really. We have an incredible calling. Jesus called us to "cure the sick, raise the dead, cleanse the lepers, and announce that God's new creation has come" in our words and in our actions. And that calling is so overwhelming that many of us lie sleeping in the bottom of the ship, wondering why the storm is so great in that "world out there." It's because we're afraid of our own power.

And we all struggle with a Jonah Complex within ourselves. We have moments when we are aware of hope welling up within us. We have moments when we feel God's creation wanting to emerge from our life story. And yet the temptation is always there—to be less, to sleep, rather than to live. Gay and lesbian people know a lot about the risk of trusting that voice within, that voice that calls for authenticity rather than just getting by. The Jonah response is to give up, to have a double life, perhaps, to fit in rather than to be who God created us to be. It's easier to choose approval than authenticity. It's easier to cut the ending short, even if it means omitting significant chapters of the story—even if it means ignoring a great calling.

There are times when we don't want to live our lives. We don't want to be us. So we're the person our neighbors, or our parents, or our teachers find easiest to deal with. And we deny our call. Workaholism is one of the most effective ways to "dress up" a Jonah Complex. We're really busy...who can question that? But we're going nowhere.

And that's one of the great ironies of trying to escape a call. As much as a call demands, it takes as much work to run away from it as it does to fulfill it. Jonah's trip to Tarshish was hardly a luxury cruise. Tarshish proved as demanding a location as Nineveh—except that it wasn't where he was supposed to be. Failure often takes as much work as success. In a book entitled, *Callings,* Gregg Levoy has outlined some ways that he thinks the Jonah Complex operates in our lives. Let me name a few of them:[4]

Hiding behind all the tasks of discernment. Do you know people who spend so much time taking personality and skill inventories that they hardly have time to do anything else? Socrates said that the unexamined life was not worth living. But the opposite is also true. The unlived life is not worth examining! There comes a point where we have to stop calculating and just dive in. We have to act on what we know, what we intuit—rather than what is empirically safe.

Waiting for the perfect moment. Waiting for the time when no one will be upset, when the transition will be without any bumps. Waiting for a financial security blanket, or the risk-free moment. There aren't any.

Telling yourself lies. "I can't afford it right now" usually means, "I won't pay for it." "It will upset my husband and he's got so much to deal with right now," often means, "I'm afraid of the conflict." Dishonesty is one of the great enablers of the Jonah Complex. When we aren't willing to pay the dues, when we're afraid of what a calling demands, we justify our fears with lies and deceptions. We blame circumstances, point the finger at others, rather than name our own anxieties and unwillingness.

Getting close, but not going all the way. The Jonah Complex is sometimes at work when you choose a path that's similar to your calling, but not quite there. You become an English teacher rather than a writer, a store manager rather than an entrepreneur.

Self-sabotage. I have a friend who has felt called to return to nursing school. He was offered a scholarship that would have paid all of his expenses and guaranteed his entrance into a program he had dreamed of for years. What happened? He forgot to get his application in by the deadline. He sabotaged himself.

Distracting yourself with other projects. My sister and her now-husband, Andy, had been together for six years, and Mary had not been in any hurry to get married. When it came time for her to get her application into Yale's School of Organization and Management, a school she'd wanted to go to since she was a kid, when it came time to apply, suddenly she decided she wanted to get married. Thank God that Andy was smart enough to say that he didn't want their marriage to be Mary's excuse for not pursuing her calling in life. They didn't get married until she had her degree in hand.

We talk ourselves out of wanting something that's important to us. You may have felt called to ordained ministry, but it feels out of reach. It demands too much schooling. You're afraid of what people will think. So you tell yourself that your present job as a nurse isn't so bad, really. You help people. The hours are stable, and you can always find a job. Work isn't everything, you rationalize. You can always help at the church in your volunteer time.

I've noticed that really tall women often tend to stand with a slight stoop. I do it myself. You know what the problem is, right? We're afraid to stand up completely straight for fear of intimidating people with how big we really are. That's a metaphor for the Jonah Complex.

I hope that this church will always see itself as a Big Place—a place where the agendas are big, where the stakes are high, where the gifts run free, and the power is obvious. I hope the agendas are nothing less than the healing of the world, the liberation of souls, the experience of the power of God Herself. I hope that our understanding of who God is can become so compelling, so energizing, so intoxicating that we don't settle for just plain, ordinary lives, rather than lives filled with the calling and the courage of God. Amen.

Rev. Cheryl Cornish
First Congregational Church, Memphis, Tennessee

About the sermon:

As I (Mary Lin) sat quietly in the pew, taking a break from an exhausting routine of research and writing, I could hardly believe my ears! I was sitting in church and listening to a woman preach about the very topic to which I had devoted long hours: listening and voice. Prophetically, Cheryl Cornish named reality in a way that moved me to reexamine my response to the call of God for my life.

Prophetic naming involves exposing the deceptive forces in our world that seek to imprison and oppress people. Sometimes, those deceptive forces take the form of systems, powerful people, language, and ideologies that are death-producing for us. At other times, those forces are internalized and people are trapped by their own thinking, deceived into denying their own value as human beings.

This sermon addresses the second form of oppression—internalized oppression. Cheryl names the ways in which these deceptions manifest themselves in everyday life. By naming the forces that seek to stifle our response to God, this sermon provides an opportunity to move beyond this way of life to new possibilities. Without prophetic naming, many of those forces would continue unnoticed or misunderstood.

This congregation is full of intelligent, well-educated people. This church maintains a policy of being open and affirming of all persons, regardless of sexual orientation, race, age, or ability. As a result, the congregation has attracted many lesbian and gay persons who had previously experienced alienation from the church. Many members are engaged in some form of social service work. The sermon is designed to challenge these gifted people to move well beyond the limitations that have been placed on them by listening more intently to the voice of God and learning to trust their own voices. We are grateful to Cheryl Cornish for allowing us to include it here.

Preaching is liberation. We speak to set people free .... There can be no redemption of the self without a liberation of the social world, and no redemption of the social world without release from the self's inner bondage. All we are saying is that preaching, as it shares God's saving purpose, will be a liberating word.

David G. Buttrick[1]

May God keep you safe until the word of your life is fully spoken.

Margaret Fuller[2]

Coda

Any reader of this book, regardless of gender, may be able to identify with certain aspects of the human experience of silence and voice. Certainly, forces working to silence women have their root in centuries of oppression and domination that grew out of ancient cultural myths about gender differences and power. Today, those same forces still exert influence, though often in subtle, more deceptive ways. Persons still compete for power. People still seek avenues of control and domination. For some people, the voices of women and others on the margins threaten these people's reign, so that they verbally (and sometimes physically) assault women and others as enemies to be subdued. The silencing of women is still a serious issue in our culture.

The issue, however, has become masked beneath a new technological veneer that has covered our lives with images and sounds and words that seem to eliminate the need for meaningful face-to-face conversation among human beings. Life on the "Web" boasts of its egalitarian benefits—language which is unburdened by gender, race, class, sexual orientation, physical ability, and so on. Even "God" has a home page. Communication in an instant by fax or e-mail has replaced the need for physical "face-to-face" intimacy that once was a natural way of life. Human beings are identified, not by the sound of their voices, but by the verification of their Social Security numbers. Our identity bar code is scanned by sensors. In many ways, the voice no longer seems to be a necessity for human beings to function within this new technological age.

Those of us who grew up with television are somewhat oblivious to the way we have learned to process reality. Children today are bombarded by images and sounds, constant stimulation that leaves them "imaginationally" challenged. Video games and computerized toys require skills of reaction and manipulation, and, at times, analysis. They do not promote, however, the exploration of interiority. They do not provide time for listening to worlds beyond the chaos of the culture.

Given the supply of language from people ready to express themselves in an instant, our world echoes with the cacophony of competing voices. Gone are the days when a person could go for long periods of time hearing only the sound of a singing bird or a crashing wave. Gone are the long afternoons in the rocking chairs on the porch, when time was filled with old stories and spaces of silence. Now, with the touch of a button or the flip of a switch, the world of sound bombards our space, affecting our consciousness with its view of reality. The voices and sounds leave an echo that repeats itself over and over in our heads, long after the original sound is silent.

In a culture where violence has trespassed upon the safety of our homes, streets, and schools, where children are killing children, and where terror awaits us on our doorstep, the sound of the lone human voice seems to have lost its power. If the voice is heard at all, it comes forth from talking heads involved in some political brawl or from public figures fabricating lies that will defend them against future consequences. We have learned to tolerate deception as a way of life, unaware that we have internalized that same deception within ourselves. No wonder our lives are so driven to succeed, to produce, to achieve, and then to retire. We are strangers to the truth within the sound of our own voices. We are no longer voices involved in meaningful conversation with God and each other. We are merely "sound bytes" in a virtual cosmos (or "chaos").

In the midst of this changing culture, the church finds itself alienated from its core activities of preaching and worship. One of the questions facing the church as it enters a new millennium is whether or not its proclamation should remain centered in the oral event of preaching. Is preaching still effective for the church's life today? As more and more generations of people encounter the world through digital image and sound, how will the church remain relevant and persuasive?

The witness of the people of God through the ages has confirmed that God is known through "voice." The power of Jesus' voice led to his identification as "the living Word." The event of Pentecost in the life of the early church opened the mouths of ordinary people for speech. Certainly, "voice" is at the heart of our faith. The "voice" is the agency of divine power. Just because "voice" has lost its impact on our visual culture, should the church abandon its fundamental claims?

The call to the church has always been a call to prophetic vocation. If the prophet is a listener who brings truth into conversation, then the vocation of the church is to foster the lively, truthful, ongoing, contemporary conversation between God and the people. Living within the covenant relationship requires the continuing work of listening and speaking within each generation. Such listening and speaking requires faith: faith that the Creator is a speaking and listening God, faith that we are made in God's image as speaking and listening beings, faith that every voice has value within its relationship with the Creator, faith that truth can emerge through meaningful conversation among voices everywhere. Such faith promotes listening and speaking as the essence of love.

Mainline Protestant churches are increasingly allowing cultural models to determine the priorities of ministry in congregations and denominations. Marketing strategies are substituted for "evangelism." Therapeutic models are substituted for new-ordered living. Success in ministry is determined by the achievement of measurable goals, rather than by the quality of authentic wonder, creativity, affection, and hope among participants in community.

During a recent conversation, a friend lamented the increasing number of churches that are terminating relationships with their pastors. In some cases, vicious smear campaigns and public attacks have been used to humiliate and stifle the pastor's voice. Churches have become so removed from authentic communication with God and each other that the "voice" of the pastor is no longer respected. Neither do they trust the potential of honest conversation as a loving means of resolving issues. In a similar way, many pastors have lost faith with their own voices, as well as the voices of their congregations, leaving them isolated and removed from authentic interaction.

Perhaps it is time for the church to return to its faith in voice. Reclaiming the power of voice may be quite difficult for the church of this modern technological age. It may be essential, though, if the church is to recover the vitality of its witness to the world.

If the church recommitted itself to a "voice-centered" theology and mission, the church would be called to take more seriously the systems and structures that stifle the voices in human community. The church would be active in opening up dialogue among the communities in which they live. That dialogue would invite and include the voices of other churches, racial/ethnic groups, social agencies, and civic organizations. At the same time, it could intentionally engage the silent and invisible persons of the community who have never been asked their opinion about anything. By providing opportunities for discussion and dialogue, the church could assist distinctive persons and groups in the difficult task of listening to each other and learning to value each differing perspective. It would tune its ear to the subtle nuances of the distinctive voices of persons, faithfully listening for the truth of God's voice within each.

The church would increase its concern for the process of integration that draws persons toward authenticity. This would mean teaching people to listen to the biblical texts with ears attuned to the divine voice, the distinctive voice of the community giving witness, and

I'm trying to voice for the laity what they might already be feeling.

SLK

the inner voice that resonates with the voice of God. In other words, it would teach people how to allow the text to speak for itself, rather than to superimpose a cultural script on the text. Emphasis would be not only on the development of one's relationship with God, but also on learning to value self and others as evidence of God's life in the world. It would also mean giving persons an opportunity to engage in the authentic expression of pain, sorrow, guilt, anger, joy, and confusion within the safety of a compassionate, listening community. A prophetic church would look for value and meaning in every voice that attempts to articulate its own experience.

The church has always played a central role in the support of artistic expression. This is not accidental, but essential to the growth and development of its spiritual life. A church that values "voice" would support all avenues of human expression that assist in a personal expression of the truth. Singing, drama, and expressive reading would allow persons to hear the sound of their own voices and encourage them to claim the power within that sound. Visual arts could give persons a means of expressing the spiritual dimension, fostering deeper discernment within community. Even filmmaking and creative writing require creativity to form first inside the human consciousness. Any medium that allows expression of human experience can assist persons in discovering an authority within themselves that has value and meaning for community.

Resistant voices would be welcomed as signals of opportunities for further work of reconciliation and liberation. Any "peace" or "unity" that denies difference is a coercive conformity that stifles the voices of God, self, and others. The "listening" church, instead, would find its vitality through mutuality, so that everyone would know safety within community and everyone could be "listened into voice."

What if "imagining, listening, and naming" became the framework out of which the church understood its own prophetic relation to the world? The same activities that bring individuals to a fuller sense of "voice" in relation to God and world could be foundational for the church as it assumes the prophetic ministry of Jesus: to "bring good news to the poor ...to proclaim release to the captives and recovery of sight to the blind, to let the oppressed go free, to proclaim the year of the LORD's favor."

The prophetic church that promotes the dynamic, contemporary conversation between persons and God would first imagine itself in the role of prophet. Churches are often paralyzed by their lack of imagination. The identities of churches are often shaped by people telling them what they cannot do, rather than by congregations getting in touch with the resources and power that belong to them. Churches with imagination can envision themselves as participants in new possibilities that shape and motivate their lives.

Prophetic churches would be listening churches. No longer content to simply repeat well-worn phrases that soothe the anxiety and tension of a changing world, churches would be listening for a *new* word in the contemporary situation. Churches would listen for the voice of God calling in the present moment to a new generation of faith. Churches would listen to the cry of the people, listening with compassion to the voices that long for the intervention of God. Churches would listen for the Spirit's breath to animate the sound of their own voices, distinctive voices for a particular context.

When the church finally discovers the sound of its own voice, the church must speak. The church's job is to name the new-ordered reality of God into the present moment, calling it into vast relief within the chaos of competing voices. The church must name oppression as it chokes the life out of people; it must also name the presence of grace within situations that seem completely hopeless; it must offer a future vision toward which we can move. The church must call forth the voices of the oppressed into an active conversation with God's voice. The church must warn those who refuse to listen to God's voice and the cries of those in need. Naming draws forth the divine reality awaiting us. The power to name is the agency of God available to God's creation, the church.

The church would not then be a sanctuary for persons wishing to escape from the world, even though it may provide the only "safe space" for some. Nor would the church pronounce edicts from a position of dominance. It would offer its words out of a deep compassion for the suffering ones. The church would invite people into a new world where the sound of their voices matter, where the sound of voice signals freedom for a dynamic, loving relationship with God and others.

Martin Luther King, Jr., spoke to the nation out of the voice of black America. Even now, male or female, the voice of the pulpit is expected to speak out of the collective voice of the people.   *RN*

In a church awakened to the importance of "voice," preaching takes on a new dynamic quality. Preaching awakens voice. The conversation does not end with the "Amen" of the preacher, but continues in the lives and voices of the ongoing conversation within community. Through preaching, people begin to trust their own experience and intuition, and learn to listen for the sound of their own voice and the voice of God.

This view of preaching is at odds with homiletic models that focus on the "word." In these contexts, preaching moves to suppress competing voices, employing courtroom rhetoric that will move the hearers to a favorable verdict. In this model, the voice of the preacher is the only voice that speaks authoritatively for God, because God speaks directly through the preacher, never engaging the personality and experience of the speaker at all. Members of the congregation remain passive recipients of the "word" of the preacher, always instructed, never consulted.

In the contemporary culture, the congregation sometimes seeks to suppress the voice of the pastor. The consumer-driven nature of American life has conditioned people to expect to get what *they* want. This mindset has been transferred to the sanctuary of the churches. If the preacher does not give them what they want, they "shop around" for another "voice" to listen to, like switching stations on the radio dial. Churches dominated by management mentality, however, often exercise their control by removing the preacher, thereby effectively silencing her voice. Within this tension, preachers find themselves "suppressed" by the expectations of a consumer audience, unable to utter an authentic or authoritative word.

Preaching that functions freely within the sound of God's voice and the human voice, however, acknowledges the grace and beauty of the preacher's voice, without claiming ultimate authority for it. The congregation values the right of the minister to speak with a distinctive, authentic voice, born out of a listening relationship to God, self, the congregation, and the world. The preacher, on the other hand, speaks in order to foster the ongoing conversation between God and humanity. The purpose of preaching is to awaken the voices of the congregation, as well as their ears, so that they may be engaged in covenant relationship with God in the present moment.

Such preaching will draw into the imagination of the congregation a new consciousness of a speaking God who listens. Preaching will reflect the skills for listening that will equip the congregation for their task. Preaching will name reality through story and metaphor so that people can articulate their own experience in new and liberating ways.

Preaching within an awareness of the sound of God's voice, then, offers hope to a church troubled with doubts about its own survival. Faith in a present, speaking God calls the church to a prophetic vocation, shaped by the work of imagining, listening, and naming. Preaching within an awareness of the importance of the human voice likewise offers hope for a new humanity freed by a love that listens all persons into speech.

In the beginning, God spoke the world into being, inviting humanity into an ongoing dialogue of mutual love. Today the dialogue continues through diverse, multiple voices of ordinary women and men coming to speech. Each voice signals the mystery and power of the divine being and honors God's creativity and love with its sound.

Finding "voice," learning to speak, is not a privilege. It is an essential part of being human. The voice puts us in touch with the source of life itself. It claims an identity fashioned by the Creator. It allows us to participate actively in the ongoing life of God. Voice is not a luxury; it is a necessity. Voice is the sound of salvation.

Appendix A

Profiles of Participants in Conversations on Voice

In Memphis, the conversation came together in a midtown restaurant. Six women participated.

Sharon Lewis Karamoko, a recent graduate of Memphis Theological Seminary, is an African American pastor of an interracial United Methodist Church in Memphis.

Cheryl Cornish, a graduate of Yale Divinity School and pastor of a growing United Church of Christ congregation in the city, has served as a solo pastor for fourteen years. She serves as a member of the Committee on Ordination for her United Church of Christ Association.

Rosalyn (Roz) Nichols is a talented preacher, teacher, and singer who serves as the associate pastor of Metropolitan Baptist Church in Memphis, a member of the Progressive National Baptist Association.

Margaret McKee, a graduate of Memphis Theological Seminary, retired recently from the position of head chaplain at the University of Tennessee Medical Center. She is the chair of the Committee on Ministry of the West Tennessee Presbytery of the Cumberland Presbyterian Church.

Almella Starks-Umoja pastors a rural African Methodist Episcopal congregation near Covington, Tennessee. A graduate of Memphis Theological Seminary, Almella is interested in pursuing further graduate work in women's history.

Mary Lin Hudson, associate professor of homiletics and worship at Memphis Theological Seminary, coordinated the meeting.

In Berkeley, a group gathered at Pacific School of Religion.

Cynthia Okayama Dopke, a recent graduate of the M.Div. program at Pacific School of Religion, is minister of church and community life at Buena Vista United Methodist Church, an Asian American congregation in Alameda, California. She is multiracial, of Japanese American and European American descent. She has special interests in community organizing.

Olivia Latu is a Pacific School of Religion student from Tonga. Her background is in early childhood development, and she feels called to parish ministry in the United Methodist Church.

Alexis Solomon is the director of Christian education at First Congregational United Church of Christ in Santa Rosa, California. She is seeking ordination in the United Church of Christ. Her interest in youth ministry and education led her to write an M.A. thesis entitled "If You're Not Outraged, You're Not Paying Attention: The Silencing of Adolescent Girls in the United States." She earned her M.Div. degree from Pacific School of Religion.

Cheryl Ward, an African American pastor of the New Liberation Community Church in Oakland, has been in ministry for more than eighteen years. With a background in Baptist and Pentecostal traditions, she is now seeking affiliation with the United Church of Christ and the Christian Church (Disciples of Christ). Cheryl graduated with an M.A. degree from Pacific School of Religion.

Appendix B

Questions for Consideration
by Conversation Groups

The following list of "theological affirmations and questions" was given to both groups of women clergy for their response:

Voice as Creative Agency of God

The Jewish-Christian canon begins with the story of creation. Through speech God brought the world into being. The voice was powerful and named all things "good." The voice signaled God's desire to be present, active, and in relationship with humanity.

Could it be that being created in the image of God means that we have the power of speaking new worlds into being? Has God authored our ability to bring an authentic and distinctive word? How do you understand God as "voice"? Is voice the primary agency of God in your experience?

Jesus—Incarnation—God in Human Speech

Christianity has taught that in Jesus, God became incarnate in human form. The Synoptic Gospels report that God verbally affirmed this at Jesus' baptism and at his transfiguration. At the site of the transfiguration, Jesus takes three disciples and ascends the mountain. He converses with Moses and Elijah, the cloud covers, and the voice of God speaks, *This is my beloved Son. Listen to him.* The story of the transfiguration, then, takes on particular significance by affirming Jesus' voice as the locus of his power and authority.

To what do you attribute the authority and power of Jesus? When you listen for the voice of Jesus what do you discover? What does it mean to "listen to his voice"? How does Jesus empower others to speak? Have you ever experienced the presence of God through human voice?

Demonic Voices

In the synagogue there was a man who had the spirit of an unclean demon, and he cried out with a loud voice, *Let us alone! What have you to do with us, Jesus of Nazareth? Have you come to destroy us? I know who you are, the Holy One of God.* But Jesus rebuked him, saying, *Be silent and come out of him!* When the demon had thrown the man down before them, he came out of the man without having done the man any harm. They were all amazed and kept saying to one another, *What kind of utterance is this? For with authority and power he commands the unclean spirits and out they come!*

Are there times when the prophetic task demands that voices must be silenced as well as awakened? By what authority are you called to silence others? When does the prophetic demand that we liberate people from the deception and captivity of external voices? How do humans distort language in a way that alienates them from each other, from God?

The Prophet—Listening and Speaking

Covenant between God and humanity is a grand drama played out through listening and through speech. The covenant relationship is always a contemporary event. The hearing, speaking, and present nature of the covenant are of one piece.

What role does the prophet play in this drama? Is the prophet ever free from the prophetic word? How does the prophetic language of hope and freedom continue to erupt?

Which Voices?

If God is understood as voice, how do we discern the distinctiveness of that voice among other voices that vie for our attention and allegiance? Can God speak through the diversity of the women and men God has created in God's image? Is it important that we recognize God's speech in its diversity? How would this affect the essence of our own speech?

Resistance to the Voice/Resistance to the New

The human voice can call redemption into being; it can demand justice. It can draw new worlds out of the old through the imagining and the naming of them. It can be resistant. God seems to choose as agents of the new creation those who have been oppressed by the old. They are often the most qualified to relate to the new and the most eager to imagine it.

To understand God as voice is to understand the breath (wind, Spirit) of God as the living quality of our own voice that conceptualizes God's word for a new place and time. The prophetic word is a fresh word, never static, but dynamic and potentially transformative.

When word is transferred from voice to print, does the nature of that word change? How has the printed Word been used both to oppose and give voice to the Holy Spirit? What are the forces in today's world that desperately seek to silence the voice of God?

Anointed for Speech

If it is true that truth sets us free, then finding our voice is an act of freedom. It allows us to participate in truth telling. The Spirit of creation anoints us for this speech.

At the baptism of Jesus it is confirmed that he is loved and acceptable. How does this kxind of affirmation foster the ministry of Jesus? How does it bring him, bring us, to voice? In what ways do people find the courage to participate in truth telling? Are there moments in which you feel more "voiced" than others? Silenced?

Bibliography

Anderson, Bernhard W. *Out of the Depths: The Psalms Speak to Us Today.* Philadelphia: Westminster Press, 1983.

Arias, Esther, and Mortimer Arias. *Cry of My People: Out of Captivity in Latin America.* New York: Friendship Press, 1991.

Bacon, Margaret Hope. *Mother of Feminism: The Story of Quaker Women in America.* San Francisco, 1986.

Baker-Fletcher, Karen. "'Soprano Obligato': the Voices of Black Women and American Conflict in the Thought of Anna Julia Cooper." In *A Troubling in My Soul.* Edited by Emilie Townes. Maryknoll, N.Y.: Orbis Books, 1993.

Barth, Karl. *The Preaching of the Gospel.* Philadelphia: Westminster Press, 1963.

_____. *Homiletics.* Louisville: Westminster/John Knox Press, 1991.

Beer, Frances. *Women and Mystical Experience in the Middle Ages.* Woodbridge, Suffolk, U.K.: Boydell Press, 1973.

Belenky, Mary Field, Blythe McVicker Clinchy, Nancy Rule Goldberger, and Jill Mattuck Tarule. *Women's Ways of Knowing: The Development of Self, Voice, and Mind.* New York: Basic, 1986.

Bellamy, V. Nelle. "Participation of Women in the Public Life of the Church from Lambeth Conference, 1867–1978." *Historical Magazine of the Protestant Episcopal Church* 51 (March 1982): 81–98.

Berkin, Carol, and Leslie Horowitz. *Women's Voices, Women's Lives: Documents of Early American History.* Boston: Northeastern University Press, 1998.

Blau, Ludwig. "Bat kol" in *Jewish Encyclopedia,* Vol. 2. New York: KTAV Publishing House, 1971–72.

Bonhoeffer, Dietrich. *Schöpfung und Fall.* München: Kaiser Verlag, 1955.

Boring, M. Eugene. *The Continuing Voice of Jesus: Christian Prophecy and the Gospel Tradition.* Louisville: Westminster/John Knox Press, 1991.

Boyd, Lois A. and R. Douglas Brackenridge. *Presbyterian Women in America: Two Centuries of a Quest for Status.* Westport, Conn.: Greenwood Press, 1983.

_____. "Questions of Power and Status: American Presbyterian Women, 1870–1980." In *Triumph Over Silence: Women in Protestant History.* Edited by R. Greaves. Westport, Conn.: Greenwood Press, 1985.

Brueggemann, Walter. *Genesis: Interpretation: A Bible Commentary for Teaching and Preaching.* Atlanta: John Knox Press, 1982.

_____. *The Meaning of the Psalms*. Minneapolis: Augsburg, 1984.

Bruno, Jordan. "Die Auferstehung Christi von den Toten in Luthers Osterpredigten, Luther: Mitteilungen der Luthergesellschaft," 1955, 13. In *Luther the Preacher*. Minneapolis: Augsburg, 1983.

Buttrick, David G. *A Captive Voice: The Liberation of Preaching*. Louisville: Westminster John Knox Press, 1994.

_____. *Homiletic: Moves and Structures*. Philadelphia: Fortress, 1987.

Carlton, Susan Brown. "Voice and the Naming of Women." In *Voices on Voice: Perspectives, Definitions, Inquiry*. Urbana, Ill: NCTE, 1994.

Chopp, Rebecca. *The Power to Speak*. New York: Crossroad, 1991.

Collins, Patricia Hill. *Black Feminist Thought: Knowledge, Consciousness, and the Politics of Empowerment, Perspectives on Power*. Vol. 2. New York: Routledge, 1991.

Craddock, Fred. *As One Without Authority*. Nashville: Abingdon, 1971.

_____. *Luke: Interpretation, A Bible Commentary for Teaching and Preaching*. Louisville: John Knox Press, 1990.

Cummins, Gail Summerskill. "Coming to Voice." In *Voices on Voice*. Urbana, Ill.: NCTE, 1994.

Dodson, Julyanne. "Nineteenth-century AME Preaching Women: Cutting Edge of Women's Inclusion in Church Polity." In *Women in New Worlds*. Edited by Hilah F. Thomas and Rosemary Skinner Keller. Nashville: Abingdon, 1981.

Donnelly, Dorothy. "Sexual Mystic: Embodied Spirituality." In *Feminist Mystic*. New York: Crossroad, 1989.

Driskill, Joseph D. *Protestant Spiritual Exercises: Theology, History, and Practice*. Morehouse, 1999.

Elkins, Heather Murray. *Worshiping Women: Reforming God's People for Praise*. Nashville: Abingdon Press, 1994.

Evans, C. F. *Saint Luke: TPI New Testament Commentaries*. Philadelphia: Trinity Press International, 1990.

Evans, James. "I Arose and Found My Voice: Black Church Studies and the Educator." In *Theological Education*, Spring, 1985, Vol. 21, No. 2.

Flinders, Carol Lee. *Enduring Grace: Living Portraits of Seven Women Mystics*. San Francisco: HarperSanFrancisco, 1993.

Fiorenza, Elisabeth Schüssler. *Bread Not Stone*. Boston: Beacon Press, 1995.

Friedman, Richard Elliott. *Anchor Bible Dictionary*, Vol. 6. New York: Doubleday, 1992.

Gifford, Carolyn de Swarte. *Women and Religion in America*. Vol. 1, *Nineteenth Century*. Edited by Rosemary Radford Ruether and Rosemary Skinner Keller. San Francisco: Harper and Row, 1981.

Gilligan, Carol, and Lyn Mikel Brown. *Meeting At the Crossroad:Women's Psychology and Girl's Development*. Cambridge, Mass.: Harvard University Press, 1992.

Gorrell, Donald K. *Women's Rightful Place:Women in United Methodist History*. Dayton: United Theological Seminary, 1980.

Hardesty, Nancy A. *Women Called to Witness: Evangelical Feminism in the Nineteenth Century*. Nashville:Abingdon, 1984.

Harrelson, Walter J. *Ten Commandments and Human Rights*. Macon, Ga.: Mercer University Press, 1997.

Harrison, Beverly Wildung, "Keeping Faith in a Sexist Church: Not for Women Only." In *Making the Connections: Essays in Feminist Social Ethics*. Edited by Carol Robb. Boston: Beacon Press, 1985.

Hassey, Janette. *No Time for Silence: Evangelical Women in Public Ministry Around the Turn of the Century*. Grand Rapids:Academie Books, 1986.

Heschel, Abraham. *God in Search of Man*. New York: Meridian Books, 1959.

Hess, Margaret Ballard. "Women's Ways of Preaching: Development of Self, Mind, and Voice in Women Preachers." D. Min. project, Andover Newton Theological School, 1994.

Hildegard of Bingen. *Scivias*. Translated by Hart, Mother Columba, and Jane Bishop. New York: Paulist Press, 1990.

Hilkert, Mary Catherine. "The Word Beneath the Words." In *The Power of Presence*. Washington, D.C.:The Pastoral Press, 1992.

_____. *Naming Grace*. New York: Continuum, 1997.

Howard, Robert. "Her Voice Will Not Be Silenced: Dynamics Within the History of Women's Preaching" (Unpublished). Quoted in Thulin, Richard, "Because of Woman's Testimony." In *Homiletic*, Vol. 21, No. 1, 1–5.

Hudson, Mary Lin. "Shall Woman Preach? Or the Question Answered: The Ministry of Louisa M. Woosley in the Cumberland Presbyterian Church, 1887–1942." Ph. D. dissertation,Vanderbilt University, 1992.

Humez, Jean McMahon. *Gifts of Power: The Writings of Rebecca Jackson, Black Visionary, Shaker Eldress*. Amherst: University of Massachusetts Press, 1993.

Isasi-Diaz,Ada Maria, andYolanda Tarango. *Hispanic Women: Prophetic Voice in the Church*. San Francisco: Harper and Row, 1988.

Jack, Dana. *Silencing the Self: Depression and Women*. Cambridge, Mass: Harvard University Press, 1991.

Jones, David A. "The Ordination of Women in the Christian Church:An Examination of the Debate, 1880–1893." *Encounter* 50, Summer (1989): 199–217.

Jordan, Judith V., Alexandra G. Kaplan, Jean Baker Miller, et al. *Woman's Growth in Connection*. New York: Guilford Press, 1991.

Julier, Laura. "Difference It Makes to Speak: The Voice of Authority in Joan Didion." In *Voices on Voice*. Urbana, Ill.: NCTE, 1994.

Kahl, Brigitte. "Materialist Reading." In *Searching the Scriptures:* Vol. 1: *A Feminist Introduction*. Edited by Elisabeth Schüssler Fiorenza. New York: Crossroad, 1993.

Keller, Rosemary Skinner. "Creating a Sphere for Women." In *Women in New Worlds*. Nashville: Abingdon, 1981.

Kuntz, Kenneth. *The Self Revelation of God*. Philadelphia: Westminster, 1967.

Long, Thomas G. *The Witness of Preaching*. Louisville: Westminster/John Knox Press, 1989.

Lorde, Audre. "Transformation into Language Action." In *Sister Outsider*. Freedom, Calif.: Crossing Press, 1984.

Luther, Martin. *Luther's Works*. St. Louis: Concordia Publishing Co., 1972.

Malina, Bruce, and Richard L. Rohrbaugh. *Social Science Commentary on the Synoptic Gospels*. Minneapolis: Fortress, 1992.

Matthews, Kenneth. *New American Commentary*, Vol. 1A. Nashville: Broadman and Holman Publishers, 1996.

McClure, John. "Conversation and Proclamation: Resources and Issues." In *Homiletic,* Summer 1997, Vol. 22 No. 1.

Menzies, Robert P. *Development of Early Christian Pneumatology with Special Reference to Luke-Acts*. Sheffield, England: Sheffield Academic Press, 1991.

Meuser, Fred W. *Luther the Preacher*. Minneapolis: Augsburg, 1983.

Miller, Patrick. *Deuteronomy: Interpretation: A Bible Commentary for Teaching and Preaching*. Louisville: John Knox Press, 1990.

Mills, Walson E., and Richard F. Wilson. *Mercer Commentary on the Bible*. Macon, Ga.: Mercer University Press, 1995.

Morton, Nelle. *Journey Is Home*. Boston: Beacon Press, 1985.

Navaretta, Mildred. "Speech." In *Grolier's Encyclopedia*. Grolier Electronic Publishing, 1993.

Neyrey, Jerome H. *Social World of Luke-Acts: Models for Interpretation*. Peabody, Mass.: Hendrickson Publishers, 1991.

Orenstein, Peggy. *School Girls*. New York: Anchor Books, Doubleday, 1994.

O'Faolain, Julia, and Lauro Martines, eds. *Not in God's Image: Women in History from the Greeks to the Victorians*. New York: Harper & Row 1973.

Ong, Walter. "Voice as Summons for Belief: Literature, Faith, and the Divided Self (1959)" In *Faith and Contexts*, Vol. 2. Edited by Thomas J. Farrell and Paul A. Soukup. Atlanta: Scholars Press, 1992.

O'Reilly, Leo. *Word and Sign in the Acts of the Apostles: A Study of Lucan Theology.* Rome: Editrice Pontificia University Georgiana, 1987.

Patrick, Dale. *The Rendering of God in the Old Testament.* Philadelphia: Fortress Press, 1981.

Petroff, Elizabeth Alvida. *Body and Soul: Essays on Medieval Women and Mysticism.* New York: Oxford University Press, 1994.

Pilch, John J. and Bruce Malina. *Biblical Social Values and Their Meaning: A Handbook.* Peabody, Mass.: Hendrickson Publishers, 1993.

Pipher, Mary. *Reviving Ophelia: Saving the Selves of Adolescent Girls.* New York: Ballantine, 1994.

Puleo, Mev. *The Struggle Is One: Voices and Visions of Liberation.* Albany: State University of New York, 1994.

Reagon, Bernice Johnson, with Bill Moyers. *The Songs Are Free.* New York: Mystic Fire Video, 1991.

Reinharz, Shulamit. "Toward an Ethnography of 'Voice' and 'Silence.'" In *Human Diversity: Perspectives on People in Context.* San Francisco: Jossey-Bass Publishers, 1994.

Reist, Benjamin A. *A Reading of Calvin's Institutes.* Louisville: Westminster/John Knox Press, 1991.

Ruether, Rosemary Radford and Rosemary Skinner Keller. *In Our Own Voices: Four Centuries of American Women's Religious Writings.* San Francisco: Harper and Row, 1995.

Rice, Charles. *Embodied Word: Preaching as Art and Liturgy.* Minneapolis: Fortress, 1991.

Rich, Adrienne. *On Lies, Secrets, and Silence: Selected Prose 1966–78.* New York: W. W. Norton & Co., 1979.

Russell, Letty M. *Church in the Round: Feminist Interpretation of the Church.* Louisville: Westminster/John Knox Press, 1993.

Sampson, Edward E. *Celebrating the Other: A Dialogic Account of Human Nature.* New York: Harvester/Wheatsheaf, 1993.

Saussy, Carroll. *God Images and Self Esteem.* Louisville: Westminster/John Knox Press, 1991.

Scarry, Elaine. *The Body in Pain: The Making and Unmaking of the World.* New York and Oxford: Oxford University Press, 1985.

Schneiders, Sandra. *The Revelatory Word.* San Francisco: Harper, 1991.

Seim, Turid Karlsen. *The Double Message: Patterns of Gender in Luke–Acts.* Nashville: Abingdon, 1994.

Sittler, Joseph. *The Anguish of Preaching.* Philadelphia: Fortress, 1966.

Smith, Archie, Jr. *Navigating the Deep River.* Cleveland: United Church Press, 1997.

_____. *The Relational Self: Ethics and Therapy from a Black Church Perspective.* Nashville: Abingdon, 1982.

Smith, Christine. "Preaching as an Art of Resistance." In *The Arts of Ministry: Feminist-Womanist Approaches.* Edited by Christine Cozad Neuger. Louisville: Westminster John Knox, 1996.

_____. *Weaving the Sermon: Preaching in a Feminist Perspective.* Louisville: Westminster/John Knox Press, 1989.

Smith, Frank J. "Petticoat Presbyterians: A Century of Debate in American Presbyterianism on the Issue of the Ordination of Women." *Westminster Theological Journal* 51, Spring (1989): 51–76.

Soelle, Dorothee. *Suffering.* Philadelphia: Fortress Press, 1975.

Strassburg, Gottfried von. *Tristan,* 13th Century, as cited in Beer's *Women and Mystical Experience in the Middle Ages.* Woodbridge, Suffolk, U.K.: Boydell Press, 1973.

Talbert, Charles H. *Literary Patterns, Theological Themes, and the Genre of Luke-Acts.* Missoula, Mont.: Scholars Press, 1974.

Taylor, Barbara Brown. *When God is Silent.* Boston: Cowley Publications, 1998.

Terrien, Samuel. *Elusive Presence: The Heart of Biblical Theology.* San Francisco: Harper and Row, 1978.

Thulin, Richard. "Because of Women's Testimony." In *Homiletic* 21 (1) Summer (1996).

Tiede, David L. *Prophecy and History in Luke-Acts.* Philadelphia: Fortress, 1980.

Tolbert, Mary Ann. "Reading for Liberation." In *Reading from This Place: Social Location and Biblical Interpretation in the United States.* Minneapolis: Fortress Press, 1995.

Torjesen, Karen Jo. *When Women Were Priests.* San Francisco: Harper, 1993.

Troeger, Thomas. *The Parable of Ten Preachers.* Nashville: Abingdon, 1993.

Turner, Mary Donovan. "Word, Words and Women." In *Serving the Table: Women in Theological Conversation.* Edited by Rita Nakashima Brock, Claudia Camp, and Serene Jones. St. Louis: Chalice Press, 1995.

Vawter, Bruce. *On Genesis: A New Reading.* Garden City, N.Y.: Doubleday & Co., 1977.

Walker, Alice. *In Search of Our Mother's Gardens.* San Diego, New York, London: Harcourt Brace Jovanovich, 1970.

Ward, Richard. *Speaking from the Heart.* Nashville: Abingdon, 1992.

Weiser, Artur. *The Psalms, Old Testament Library.* London: SCM Press, 1962.

Westermann, Claus. *Basic Forms of Prophetic Speech.* Philadelphia: Westminster Press, 1967.

Wetherilt, Ann Kirkus. *That They May Be Many: Voices of Women, Echoes of God*. New York: Continuum, 1994.

Whitehead, Alfred. *Religion in the Making*. New York: Macmillan, 1926.

Willard, Frances. *Woman in the Pulpit*. Boston: D. Lathrop Company, 1888.

_____. *Writing Out My Heart*. Edited by Carolyn De Swarte Gifford. Urbana and Chicago: University of Illinois Press, 1995.

Williams, Michael. *Storyteller's Companion to the Bible:* Vol 6. *The Pre-Exilic Prophets*. Nashville: Abingdon Press, 1996.

Winter, Miriam Therese, Adair Lummis, and Allison Stokes. *Defecting In Place*. New York: Crossroad, 1994.

Woosley, Louisa M. *Shall Woman Preach? Or the Question Answered*. Caneyville, Ky.: 1981.

Yancey, Kathleen Blake. *Voices on Voice: Perspectives, Definitions, Inquiry*. Urbana, Ill.: NCTE, 1994.

Zikmund, Barbara Brown, Adair T. Lummis, and Patricia Mei Yin Chang. *Clergy Women: An Uphill Calling*. Louisville: Westminster John Knox Press, 1998.

Zum Brunn, Emilie, and Georgette Epincy-Burgard. *Woman in Medieval Europe*. New York: Paragon House, 1989.

Notes

Introduction

[1]For more information about metaphors, see Gibson Winter, *Liberating Creation: Foundations of Religious Social Ethics* (New York: The Crossroad Publishing Company, 1981); George Lakoff and Mark Johnson, *Metaphors We Live By* (Chicago: The University of Chicago Press, 1980); Sallie McFague, *Metaphorical Theology: Models of God in Religious Language* (Philadelphia: Fortress Press, 1982).

Chapter 1. Voice as Emerging Metaphor

[1]Martin Luther, *Luther's Works* (St. Louis: Concordia Publishing House, 1972), 339.

[2]Walter Ong, "Voice as Summons for Belief: Literature, Faith and the Divided Self (1959)," in *Faith and Contexts:* Vol. 2, ed. Thomas J. Farrell and Paul A. Soukup (Atlanta: Scholars Press, 1992), 72.

[3]Ibid., 68.

[4]Nelle Morton, *The Journey Is Home* (Boston: Beacon Press, 1985), 87.

[5]Alfred Whitehead regarded speech as human nature itself. "Expression," he said, "is the one fundamental sacrament." See *Religion in the Making* (New York: Macmillan, 1926), 131.

[6]Mildred Navaretta, "Speech," *Grolier's Encyclopedia* (Grolier Electronic Publishing, 1993).

[7]Edward Sampson talks about the different voices through which we speak and relate to the world, our many voices of thinking and knowing. See Edward E. Sampson, *Celebrating the Other: A Dialogic Account of Human Nature* (New York: Harvester/Wheatsheaf, 1993), 213.

[8]Kathleen Blake Yancey, ed., *Voice on Voice: Perspectives, Definitions, Inquiry* (Urbana, Ill.: National Council of Teachers of English, 1994), viii.

[9]Ada Maria Isasi-Diaz and Yolanda Tarango, *Hispanic Women: Prophetic Voice in the Church* (San Francisco: Harper and Row, 1988), xvi.

[10]Yancey, *Voices on Voice,* ix.

[11]Ibid., xix.

[12]Adrienne Rich, *On Lies, Secrets, and Silence: Selected Prose 1966–1978* (Boston: Beacon Press, 1985).

[13]Rosemary Radford Ruether and Rosemary Skinner Keller, eds., *In Our Own Voices: Four Centuries of American Women's Religious Writings* (San Francisco: Harper and Row, 1995), 2.

[14]Doug Bailey, sermon preached in the chapel at Memphis Theological Seminary, 1997.

[15]Bernice Johnson Reagon: with Bill Moyers, *The Songs Are Free* (New York: Mystic Fire Video, 1991).

[16]Patricia Hill Collins, *Black Feminist Thought: Knowledge, Consciousness, and the Politics of Empowerment, Perspectives on Power,* Vol. 2 (New York: Routledge, 1991), 93–95.

[17]Karen Baker-Fletcher, "'Soprano Obligato': The Voices of Black Women and American Conflict in the Thought of Anna Julia Cooper," in *A Troubling in My Soul,* ed. Emilie M. Townes (Maryknoll, N.Y.: Orbis Books, 1993), 184.

[18]Susan Brown Carlton, "Voice and the Naming of Women," in *Voices on Voice,* ed. Yancey, 226.

[19]Esther Arias and Mortimer Arias, *The Cry of My People: Out of Captivity in Latin America* (New York: Friendship Press, 1991), 87–88.

[20]Mev Puleo, *The Struggle is One: Voices and Visions of Liberation* (Albany: State University of New York, 1994), 9–10.

[21]Ibid., 10.

[22]Mary Field Belenky, Blythe McVicker Clinchy, Nancy Rule Goldberger, and Jill Mattuck Tarule, *Women's Ways of Knowing: The Development of Self, Voice, and Mind* (New York: Basic Books, 1986), 18.

[23]Shulamit Reinharz, "Toward an Ethnography of 'Voice' and 'Silence,'" in *Human Diversity: Perspectives on People in Context* (San Francisco: Jossey-Bass Publishers, 1994), 181.

Chapter 2. Created in the Sound of God: Voice in the Old Testament

[1]Barbara Brown Taylor, *When God is Silent* (Boston: Cowley Publications, 1998), 3.

[2]Abraham Heschel, *God in Search of Man* (New York: Farrar, Strauss, and Cudalhy, 1955), 275.

[3]Dorothee Soelle, *Suffering* (Philadelphia: Fortress Press, 1975), 75.

[4]This story alerts us to the distinctiveness of this God. Rarely in other ancient Near Eastern mythic creation accomplished through the uttered word. Bruce Vawter, *On Genesis: A New Reading* (Garden City, N.Y.: Doubleday & Co., 1977), 42. Kenneth Matthews, *Genesis,* New American Commentary 1A (Nashville, Tenn.: Broadman and Holman Publishers, 1996), 117ff., contrasts the spoken word of the God in Genesis with those of the gods of Egypt and Mesopotamia.

[5]Nelle Morton, *The Journey is Home* (Boston: Beacon Press, 1985), 89. Morton discusses the root form for *ruach.* It derives, she says from the word breath, breath of the body, breath of life, wind of the cosmos. The word *ruach* is, in Hebrew, in the feminine gender. In its ancient usage, breath [spirit] was thought to be provided by the mother at birth. The early Goddess was the source and nurturer of all living. The ancient history of the understanding of spirit is seen as a thread of the feminine running through patriarchal literature.

[6]See Dale Patrick, *The Rendering of God in the Old Testament* (Philadelphia: Fortress Press, 1981), 90ff. He engages in a discussion of the speaking/acting God. Patrick speaks to the artificial dualism created by some who would divide the activity of God into the artificial categories of word and deed. God's speaking, he indicates, is a force itself in the world; it establishes God's presence. Speech is a divine intervention that accomplishes something in its own right.

[7]See vv. 1, 3, 5, 6, 8, 9, 10, 11, 14, 20, 22, 24, 26, 28, 29. Walter Brueggemann, *Genesis,* Interpretation: A Bible Commentary for Teaching and Preaching (Atlanta: John Knox Press, 1982), 24.

[8]As in v. 15 where the greater light is created to rule the day and the lesser to rule the night. God also names the day, the night, sky, earth, and seas.

[9]While in v. 22 God blesses the creatures of sea and air, in v. 28 God blesses male and female and says explicitly to them, "Be fruitful and multiply..."

[10]For an interesting perspective on voice and deity, see Elaine Scarry, *The Body in Pain: The Making and Unmaking of the World* (New York and Oxford: Oxford University

Press, 1985), 200–206. She sees God as a bodiless voice and people as a voiceless body. To have a body is to be describable, creatable, alterable, woundable. To have only a voice is none of these things.

[11]See, for instance, Psalm 33:6, 9.

[12]See, for example:Psalms 3:4; 5:2,3; 6:8; 26:7; 27:7; 28:2,6; 31:22; 42:4,7; 55:17; 64:1; 66:19; 77:1; 86:6; 116:1; 119:149; 130:2; 140:6; 141:1; 142:1.

[13]Scholars have analyzed and described the form of the lament psalms with different language and theological emphases. See, for instance, the outline provided by Bernhard W. Anderson in *Out of the Depths: The Psalms Speak to Us Today* (Philadelphia: Westminster Press, 1983), 95ff. Anderson describes the structure of the lament as Address to God, Complaint, Confession of Trust, Petition, Words of Assurance, Vow of Praise. Westermann's analysis is also representative and demonstrates the dramatic movement from the call to God to hear the despair to the assurance that God listens, cares, saves. Westermann sees this as the movement from "plea" to "praise." As quoted in Walter Brueggemann, *The Meaning of the Psalms* (Minneapolis: Augsburg, 1984), 54.

[14]Artur Weiser, *The Psalms*, Old Testament Library (London: SCM Press, 1962), 260–261.

[15]See these psalms, which also attest to the mighty strength of God's voice. "The LORD also thundered in the heavens and the Most High uttered his voice" (18:13). "The nations are in an uproar, the kingdoms totter; he utters his voice, the earth melts" (46:6). "O rider in the heavens, the ancient heavens; listen, he sends out his voice, his mighty voice" (68:33).

[16]Terrien analyzes the two stories that can be discerned behind the repetitions and discrepancies in the texts that relate the story of deliverance from Egypt and the Sinai theophanies in particular. In the Elohist strand of Northern Israel, the hearing of sounds and voices is stressed. These interpretations were followed by the Deuteronomists, who interpreted events in a similar way. On the other hand, the Yahwist theologians from Judah stressed visions of divine glory. Terrien discusses the conflict between ear and eye that persisted throughout the centuries in biblical times and which continues, in modified fashion, in Judaism and Christianity today. See Samuel Terrien, *The Elusive Presence: The Heart of Biblical Theology* (San Francisco: Harper & Row, 1978), 121.

[17]Ibid., 60–69. According to Terrien, in this story the visual manifestation of Yahweh's presence is soon absorbed by the spoken word. The Hebraic theophany is more heard than seen. Speech allows for give and take and interaction between God and humanity. This theology of speech is, then, a theology of presence. Kuntz also acknowledges that in theophanic encounter, the visual act of seeing subtly passes into the act of hearing. He defines a theophany as a temporal manifestation of the deity to humanity involving visible and audible elements that signal God's presence. See Kenneth Kuntz, *The Self Revelation of God* (Philadelphia: Westminster Press, 1967), 17, 40.

[18]The word "Deuteronomy" means "second law." It is a second hearing, so to speak, of Sinai.

[19]Dale Patrick, *The Rendering of God in the Old Testament* (Philadelphia: Fortress, 1981), 93.

[20]Walter Harrelson acknowledges that the Decalogue was at first vocal, spoken. The words were vital links between God and people. See Walter J. Harrelson, *The Ten Commandments and Human Rights* (Macon, Ga.: Mercer University Press, 1997), 135.

[21]Patrick Miller, *Deuteronomy,* Interpretation (Louisville, Ky.: John Knox Press, 1990), 67.

[22]Memory is a recognition of what was alive and meaningful in the past and is still vibrant in the present. See Watson E. Mills, Richard F. Wilson, eds., *Mercer Commentary on the Bible* (Macon, Ga.: Mercer University Press, 1995).

[23]For references to "Voice of the word" see Psalms 103:20; 106:25; Exodus 36:6. In Exodus 36:6 the NRSV reads: " ...and word was proclaimed throughout the camp." In Hebrew this reads: "Moses...caused his voice to pass among the people."

[24]Though the relationship between the tent of meeting and the tabernacle is uncertain, the tent of meeting was the location of revelation as the people traveled through the wilderness. See Richard Elliott Friedman, "Tabernacle" in *Anchor Bible Dictionary,* Vol. 6, ed. David Noel Freedman (New York: Doubleday, 1992), 292–300.

[25]Terrien, *The Elusive Presence,* 175–178.

[26]Heschel, *God in Search of Man,* 146.

[27]This is not unlike the process that preserved the various testimonies in the gospels. Their various forms point to the continual reinterpretation of these sayings in the post-Easter church to express the continuing word of Jesus to the church in changed circumstances. See M. Eugene Boring, *The Continuing Voice of Jesus: Christian Prophecy and the Gospel Tradition* (Louisville, Ky.: Westminster/John Knox Press, 1991), 15–16.

[28]See Psalm 115:5; 135:16; Jeremiah 10:5, which speak about idols that do not speak.

[29]See 11:18—12:6; 15:10–21; 17:5–10, 14–18; 18:18–23; 20:7–18.

[30]See, for instance, chapter 3:11–14 where the fourfold repetition of "says the LORD" reminds the community that it is Yahweh calling them to return (v. 12), bringing a word of mercy (v. 12), reminding them of their lack of obedience (v. 13), and again calling them to return (v. 14). This is just one more rhetorical strategy by which the prophet legitimizes what he says and substantiates for the community that he has the right to speak. For a discussion of the messenger formula, see Claus Westermann, *Basic Forms of Prophetic Speech* (Philadelphia: Westminster Press, 1967), 90–128.

[31]Abraham Heschel, *God in Search of Man,* 259–60.

[32]Michael Williams, ed., *The Storyteller's Companion to the Bible: The Pre-Exilic Prophets,* Vol. 6 (Nashville, Tenn.: Abingdon Press, 1996), 90.

[33]Esther and Mortimer Arias, *The Cry of My People* (New York: Friendship Press, 1980), 114.

[34]Of interest is the Hebrew term *bat qol,* translated literally in English "daughter of a voice." This *bat qol* was the heavenly or divine voice that revealed God's will to humanity. According to rabbinic tradition the *bat qol* was already heard during the biblical period (proclaiming Tamar's innocence, validating Solomon's judgment in awarding the child to the true mother, etc). "Voice" then, as "daughter of a voice," was the phrase used to depict God's active presence with the Israelite people after the biblical period of prophecy. See Ludwig Blau, "bat kol" in *Jewish Encyclopedia,* Vol. 2 (New York: KTAV Publishing House, 1971–72).

Chapter 3. The Power to Speak: Voice in the New Testament

[1]Heschel, *God in Search of Man,* 174.

[2]Sandra Schneiders, *The Revelatory Word* (San Francisco: Harper, 1991), 75.

[3]Robert Menzies argues convincingly that the portrayal of the gift of the Spirit in Luke-Acts is consistent with the Jewish perspective of the Spirit as the source of prophetic endowment that enables its recipient to proclaim the coming realm of God. This reflects a "prophetic pneumatology" that is at odds with a distinctively Pauline pneumatology that is soteriological in character. For a thorough discussion of the issues, see Robert P. Menzies, *The Development of Early Christian Pneumatology with Special Reference to Luke-Acts* (Sheffield, England: Sheffield Academic Press, 1991).

[4]Bruce Malina and Richard L. Rohrbaugh, *Social Science Commentary on the Synoptic Gospels* (Minneapolis: Fortress Press, 1992), 284.

[5]"A woman's position in her husband's family was never secure until she bore a son. Only then did she have a 'blood' relationship that secured her place." Ibid., 287.

[6]"Travel [by women] for other than customary reasons was often considered deviant behavior in antiquity" (ibid., 291).

[7]Malina and Rohrbaugh (294) list qualities of Middle Eastern women's poetry as more extemporaneous and informal, often dealing with subjects that are forbidden to be discussed in the public sphere (e.g., conception). The tone is deeply emotional concerning these private subjects.

[8]Ibid., 291. The issue of the private vs. the public realm is a central issue in Luke-Acts. The blending of the public religious life within the private households of Jesus' followers offered the potential of equality for women, who had authority in the private realm. On the other hand, the demands for subordination of women may have been intensified to some extent as the rigid patriarchy of public culture that reinforced a patriarchal structure within the household. Turid Karlsen Seim, *The Double Message: Patterns of Gender in Luke-Acts* (Nashville, Tenn.: Abingdon Press, 1994), 125.

[9]Brigitte Kahl, "Materialist Reading," in *Searching the Scriptures,* Vol. 1: *A Feminist Introduction,* ed. by Elisabeth Schüssler Fiorenza (New York: Crossroad, 1993), 238.

[10]The patriarchal culture expected the father to name the child as confirmation of paternity.

[11]His speech in Luke 1 is a good example of the poetry of that day in the public sphere. "To be able to quote the tradition from memory, to apply it in creative or appropriate ways to the situations of daily living, not only brings honor to the speaker, but lends authority to his words, as well. The song of Zechariah, the so-called *Benedictus,* in Luke 1:68–79 is an example." It draws upon traditional sources (Psalms 41, 111, 132, 105, 106, and Micah 7), constructing phrases into a new poem befitting a special occasion. See Malina and Rohrbaugh, *Social Science Commentary,* 293–294.

[12]Seim, *The Double Message,* 176–179.

[13]Menzies cites the early rabbinic literature, Sota 13.3, "When the latter prophets died, that is, Haggai, Zechariah, and Malachi, then the Holy Spirit came to an end in Israel. But even so, they made them hear [heavenly messages] through an echo." Menzies, *The Development of Early Christian Pneumatology,* 92–96.

[14]John J. Pilch and Bruce J. Malina, *Biblical Social Values and Their Meaning: A Handbook* (Peabody, Mass.: Hendrickson Publishers, 1993), 126–128.

[15]The "adoption" theory claims that through Jesus' anointing at Jordan, Jesus' sonship is perfected and completed. It marked a new and deeper existential awareness of God as Father, thus assuming the full identity of son and Messiah at his baptism. See Menzies, *The Development of Early Christian Pneumatology,* 152.

¹⁶Menzies prefers to think of Jesus' baptism as signaling the beginning of his messianic ministry, but not altering his essential relation to God (149–154).

¹⁷A connection between Luke 4 and Deuteronomy 18:15f. is suggested as evidence of Jesus' prophetic calling by David L. Tiede, *Prophecy and History in Luke-Acts* (Philadelphia: Fortress, 1980), 40–43.

¹⁸Malina and Rohrbaugh, *Social Science Commentary,* 329–330.

¹⁹Fred B. Craddock, *Luke,* Interpretation: A Bible Commentary for Teaching and Preaching (Louisville: John Knox Press, 1990), 95–98.

²⁰Could this be a foreshadowing of the prophetic speech of the early Christian community, a community that was restored to life at Jesus' resurrection?

²¹Craddock, *Luke,* 133–134.

²²At the end of Luke's Gospel, this instruction is brought to fulfillment when the stranger engages the two disciples in conversation about "Moses and the prophets" on the road to Emmaus (Luke 24:13–35).

²³Craddock, *Luke,* 228.

²⁴C. F. Evans, *Saint Luke,* TPI New Testament Commentaries (Philadelphia: Trinity Press International, 1990), 682.

²⁵Commemorating the giving of the Law at Mount Sinai could have been part of the festival at the time, because this emphasis emerges during celebrations after the destruction of the temple. Leo O'Reilly, *Word and Sign in the Acts of the Apostles: A Study in Lucan Theology* (Rome: Editrice Pontificia Universita Gregoriana, 1987), 18–21. Menzies uses the same historical evidence, however, to deny any intrinsic connection between the events of the early Christian Pentecost and the giving of the Law at Mount Sinai.

²⁶O'Reilly, 22–23.

²⁷Charles H. Talbert, *Literary Patterns, Theological Themes, and the Genre of Luke-Acts* (Missoula, Mont.: Scholars Press, 1974), 16.

²⁸Jerome H. Neyrey, ed., *The Social World of Luke-Acts: Models for Interpretation* (Peabody, Mass.: Hendrickson Publishers, 1991), 357.

²⁹Malina and Rohrbaugh, 292–293.

³⁰It would be difficult to exploit the girl economically if she were free to speak from her own reality.

³¹"The movement away from the temple is at the same time a movement towards the house…an alternative to the temple and its lust for power, also an alternative to the social control exercised by the public sphere of the city" (Seim, 139, 145).

Chapter 4. Commitment to Conversation: An Emerging Theology of Voice

¹Francis E. Willard, *Writing Out My Heart,* ed. Carolyn De Swarte Gifford (Urbana and Chicago: University of Illinois Press, 1995), 129.

²Barbara Brown Taylor, *When God is Silent* (Boston: Cowley Publications, 1998), 118.

³David G. Buttrick, *A Captive Voice: The Liberation of Preaching* (Louisville Ky.: Westminster/John Knox Press, 1994), 32.

⁴Thomas G. Long, *The Witness of Preaching* (Louisville, Ky.: Westminster/John Knox Press, 1989), 24–30.

⁵Karl Barth, *The Preaching of the Gospel.* Trans. B. E. Hooke (Philadelphia: Westminster, 1963), 12.

⁶Benjamin A. Reist, *A Reading of Calvin's Institutes* (Louisville: Westminster/John Knox Press, 1991), 98.

⁷Bruno Jordan,"Die Auferstehung Christi von den Toten in Luthers Osterpredigten," *Luther: Mitteilungen der Luthergesellschaft,* 1955, 13. As quoted in Fred W. Meuser, *Luther the Preacher* (Minneapolis: Augsburg, 1983), 12.

⁸Karl Barth, *Homiletics* (Louisville: Westminster/John Knox Press, 1991), 47–55.

⁹Fred Craddock, *As One Without Authority* (Nashville: Abingdon Press, 1971).

¹⁰Ibid., 24–50.

¹¹Ann Kirkus Wetherilt, *That They May Be Many: Voices of Women, Echoes of God* (New York: Continuum, 1994), 140–142.

¹²Richard Thulin, "Because of Women's Testimony..." in *Homiletic,* Summer, 1996, 3.

¹³Frances Willard, *Woman in the Pulpit* (Boston: D. Lathrop Company, 1888), 21.

¹⁴Richard Ward, *Speaking from the Heart: Preaching with Passion* (Nashville: Abingdon, 1992), 85.

¹⁵Thomas Troeger, *The Parable of Ten Preachers* (Nashville: Abingdon, 1992), 11.

¹⁶Charles Rice, *The Embodied Word: Preaching as Art and Liturgy* (Minneapolis: Fortress, 1991), 127–128.

¹⁷See Joseph Sittler, *The Anguish of Preaching* (Philadelphia: Fortress, 1966).

¹⁸Christine Smith, *Weaving the Sermon: Preaching in a Feminist Perspective* (Louisville: Westminster/John Knox Press, 1989), 52.

¹⁹Robert Howard, "Her Voice will Not be Silenced: Dynamics Within the History of Women's Preaching." Unpublished paper as quoted in Richard Thulin's "Because of Woman's Testimony..." in *Homiletic* 21: 1, 1–5.

Chaper 5. Context and Voice: Stories from History

¹Christine Smith, *Weaving the Sermon,* 99.

²Rebecca Chopp, *The Power to Speak* (New York: Crossroad, 1991), 6.

³Although the new order set aside cultural barriers that had divided communities, other traditions remained intact. In the practical realm, women were still expected to perform those duties assigned to their gender for the benefit of the larger household. And so the women prepared to anoint the body of Jesus for burial. Malina and Rohrbaugh, *Social Science Commentary,* 410.

⁴Throughout the narrative of Luke, the author uses figures in dazzling clothes to signify an event of spiritual importance. The reader encounters such persons elsewhere in the stories of the transfiguration and ascension of Jesus. Craddock, *Luke,* 281–282.

⁵Seim, *The Double Message,* 150–154.

⁶Ibid., 155–156.

⁷Ibid., 156–157.

⁸Ibid., 1–3.

⁹Frances Beer, *Women and Mystical Experience in the Middle Ages* (Woodbridge, Suffolk, U.K.: Boydell Press, 1992), 2.

¹⁰Ibid., 3.

¹¹Beer cites the works of German Gottfried von Strassburg in *Tristan,* a thirteenth-century romance and a French work, "Coutumes de Beauvaisis" found in *Not in God's Image: Women in History from the Greeks to the Victorians,* ed. Julia O'Faolain and Lauro Martines (New York: Harper and Row, 1973).

[12]For a profile of these and other medieval mystics, see Carol Lee Flinders, *Enduring Grace: Living Portraits of Seven Women Mystics* (San Francisco: HarperSanFrancisco, 1993).

[13]Elizabeth Alvilda Petroff, *Body and Soul: Essays on Medieval Women and Mysticism* (New York: Oxford University Press, 1994), 11.

[14]Emilie Zum Brunn and Georgette Epiney-Burgard, *Women Mystics in Medieval Europe* (New York: Paragon House, 1989), 9–10.

[15]Hildegard of Bingen, *Scivias*, trans. Mother Columba Hart and Jane Bishop (New York: Paulist Press, 1990), 59.

[16]Ibid., 60.

[17]Ibid., 11.

[18]Ibid., 60-61.

[19]Beer, *Women and Mystical Experience,* 19–20.

[20]Petroff, *Body and Soul,* 12.

[21]Beer, *Women and Mystical Experience,* 24.

[22]Hildegard, *Scivias,* 19.

[23]Ibid., 77.

[24]Ibid., 278.

[25]Beer, *Women and Mystical Experience,* 24.

[26]Nancy A. Hardesty, *Women Called to Witness: Evangelical Feminism in the Nineteenth Century* (Nashville: Abingdon, 1984); Janette Hassey, *No Time for Silence: Evangelical Women in Public Ministry around the Turn of the Century* (Grand Rapids, Mich.: Academie Books, 1986).

[27]Carolyn de Swarte Gifford, "Women in Social Reform Movements," in *Women and Religion in America,* ed. Rosemary Radford Ruether and Rosemary Skinner Keller, Vol. 1. *The Nineteenth Century* (San Francisco: Harper & Row, 1981).

[28]Margaret Hope Bacon, *Mothers of Feminism: The Story of Quaker Women in America* (San Francisco: Harper & Row, 1986), 107–108.

[29]For a discussion of the controversy of women's ordination in mainline Protestant churches, see Frank J. Smith, "Petticoat Presbyterians: a Century of Debate in American Presbyterianism on the Issue of the Ordination of Women," *The Westminster Theological Journal* 51 (Spring 1989): 51–76; David A. Jones, "The Ordination of Women in the Christian Church: an Examination of the Debate, 1880–1893," *Encounter* 50 (Summer 1989): 199–217; Lois A. Boyd and R. Douglas Brackenridge, "Questions of Power and Status: American Presbyterian Women, 1870–1980," in *Triumph Over Silence: Women in Protestant History,* ed. R. Greaves (Westport, Conn.: Greenwood Press, 1985); V. Nelle Bellamy, "Participation of Women in the Public Life of the Church from Lambeth Conference 1867–1978," *Historical Magazine of the Protestant Episcopal Church* 51 (March 1982): 81–98; Julyanne Dodson, "Nineteenth Century AME Preaching Women: Cutting Edge of Women's Inclusion in Church Polity," in *Women in New Worlds,* ed. Hilah F. Thomas and Rosemary Skinner Keller (Nashville: Abingdon, 1981), 276–289; Rosemary Skinner Keller, "Creating a Sphere for Women," in *Women in New Worlds,* 246–260; Donald K. Gorrell, ed., *Women's Rightful Place: Women in United Methodist History* (Dayton, Ohio: United Theological Seminary, 1980).

[30]Lois A. Boyd and R. Douglas Brackenridge, *Presbyterian Women in America: Two Centuries of a Quest for Status* (Westport, Conn.: Greenwood Press, 1983), 91–156.

[31]The following information about Louisa M. Woosley is taken from Mary Lin Hudson's doctoral dissertation entitled *Shall Woman Preach? Or the Question Answered: The*

Ministry of Louisa M. Woosley in the Cumberland Presbyterian Church, 1887–1942 (Nashville : Vanderbilt University, 1992).

[32]Louisa M. Woosley, *Shall Woman Preach? Or the Question Answered* (Caneyville, Ky.: 1981). This book was reprinted by the Cumberland Presbyterian Church Board of Christian Education in 1989 in honor of the 100th anniversary of her ordination.

[33]Ibid., 96.

[34]Ibid., 97.

[35]Her descendants remember the story told of how her family had prepared a casket for her, expecting her to die any moment.

[36]Ibid., 97–98.

[37]Ibid., 98.

[38]Ibid., 100.

[39]Ibid., 101.

[40]Beverly Wildung Harrison, *Making the Connections: Essays in Feminist Social Ethics,* ed. Carol S. Robb (Boston: Beacon Press, 1985).

[41]Ibid., 207.

[42]Ibid., 209.

[43]Ibid.

[44]Ibid., 210.

[45]Ibid.

[46]Ibid., 213.

[47]Ibid., 213–214.

Chapter 6. To Be Saved from Silence

[1]Yancey, *Voices on Voice,* xix.

[2]Adrienne Rich, *On Lies, Secrets, and Silence: Selected Prose 1966–78,* 193.

[3]Alice Walker, *In Search of Our Mother's Gardens* (San Diego, New York, London: Harcourt Brace Jovanovich, 1970), 16.

[4]Laura Julier, "The Difference It Makes to Speak: The Voice of Authority in Joan Didion," in *Voices on Voice: Perspectives, Definitions, Inquiry,* ed. Kathleen Blake Yancey (Urbana, Ill: National Council of Teachers of English, 1994), 130.

[5]Carol Gilligan and Lyn Mikel Brown, *Meeting at the Crossroads: Women's Psychology and Girl's Development* (Cambridge, Mass: Harvard University Press, 1992).

[6]Peggy Orenstein, *School Girls* (New York: Anchor Books, Doubleday, 1994), xvi.

[7]Mary Pipher, *Reviving Ophelia: Saving the Selves of Adolescent Girls* (New York: Ballantine, 1994).

[8]Mary Field Belenky, Blythe McVicker Clinchy, Nancy Rule Goldberger, and Jill Mattuck Tarule, *Women's Ways of Knowing* (New York: Basic Books, 1986).

[9]Archie Smith, Jr., *Navigating the Deep River* (Cleveland, Ohio: United Church Press, 1997), 37.

[10]Archie Smith, Jr., *The Relational Self: Ethics and Therapy from a Black Church Perspective* (Nashville, Tenn.: Abingdon, 1982), 15.

[11]Many women fear using power in any way other than helping others. For many women it becomes more comfortable simply to feel inadequate. To feel otherwise threatens the woman with the possibility that power and authority have the potential to be destructive. Some believe that using this power will destroy their sense of identity. See

Judith V. Jordan, Alexandra G. Kaplan, Jean Baker Miller, Irene P. Stiver, and Janet L. Surrey, *Women's Growth in Connection* (New York: The Guilford Press, 1991), 2–3.

[12]Dana Jack, *Silencing the Self: Depression and Women* (Cambridge, Mass.: Harvard University Press, 1991), 32.

[13]Miriam Therese Winter, Adair Lummis, and Allison Stokes, *Defecting in Place* (New York: Crossroad, 1994), 201.

[14]Adrienne Rich, *Lies, Secrets, and Silence* (New York: W. W. Norton & Company, 1979), 9–11.

[15]Ibid.

[16]Winter et al., *Defecting in Place,* 9.

[17]Ibid., 65.

[18]Ibid., 48.

[19]Ibid., 19.

[20]Ibid., 10.

[21]Ibid., 105.

[22]Margaret Ballard Hess, *Women's Ways of Preaching: Development of Self, Mind, and Voice in Women Preachers,* D.Min. Project (Andover, Mass.: Newton Theological School, May 1994), 83–84. For a more complete understanding of the ways the church began to silence women and discourage them from taking leadership roles, see Karen Jo Torjesen, *When Women Were Priests* (San Francisco: Harper, 1993).

[23]Chopp, *The Power to Speak,* 3. See also, Dorothy Donnelly "The Sexual Mystic: Embodied Spirituality," in *The Feminist Mystic,* ed. Mary E. Giles (New York: Crossroad, 1989), 120–141. Karen Jo Torjesen discusses the historical conversation about women's bodies, their association with sexuality and the ultimate suspicion that became associated with them in *When Women Were Priests.* Heather Murray Elkins also speaks about the powerful taboo that prevents the intimate connection between women's bodies and word in *Worshiping Women: Reforming God's People for Praise* (Nashville: Abingdon Press, 1994), 94.

[24]Chopp, *The Power to Speak,* 24.

[25]Carroll Saussy, *God Images and Self Esteem* (Louisville: Westminster/John Knox Press, 1991), 12.

[26]Information about Anna Julia Cooper found in "'Soprano Obligato': The Voices of Black Women and American Conflict in the Thought of Anna Julia Cooper," by Karen Baker-Fletcher in *A Troubling in My Soul.* ed. Emilie M. Townes (Maryknoll, N.Y.: Orbis Books, 1993), 172–185.

[27]This understanding holds much in common with *minjung* theology. Here a process of coming to voice is described in redemptive ways. Human beings are originally the word (freedom). It is suppressed (silenced). Then *hen* arises and comes up (resurrects) as a rumor and then becomes the storm (revolution). *Minjung* theology arises out of stories of suffering and hope. To know *minjung* theology is to know what it means to be a voiceless Korean in one's own land. Suffering can be repressed either by one's own self or through oppression. The unjust situation of oppression can be cured only when the structures of society change.

[28]Gail Summerskill Cummins, "Coming to Voice," in *Voices on Voice,* 49.

[29]Chopp, *The Power to Speak,* 4.

[30]Audre Lorde, "The Transformation into Language in Action," *Sister Outsider* (Freedom, Calif.: The Crossing Press, 1984), 40.

[31]RichardThulin,"Because ofWoman'sTestimony," *Homiletic* 21:1 (Summer, 1996): 3.

[32]Mary Catherine Hilkert, "TheWord Beneath theWords" in *The Power of Presence* (Washington, D.C.:The Pastoral Press, 1992), 49–70.

[33]See Mary Catherine Hilkert, *Naming Grace* (NewYork: Continuum, 1997), 169–171.

[34]Barbara Brown Zikmund,AdairT. Lummis,Patricia MeiYin Chang, *ClergyWomen: An Uphill Calling* (Louisville:Westminster John Knox Press, 1998), 111–113.

Chapter 7. Coming to Voice

[1]Heather Murray Elkins, *Worshiping Women: Reforming God's People for Praise* (Nashville:Abingdon Press, 1994), 94.

[2]Mary AnnTolbert, "Reading for Liberation," in *Reading from this Place: Social Location and Biblical Interpretation in the United States,* Vol. 1, Fernando F. Segovia and Mary Ann Tolbert, eds. (Minneapolis: Fortress, 1995), 263.

[3]Max Picard, *The World of Silence,* trans. Staley Goldman (Chicago: Henry Regency, 1952), 26–27, as quoted in Fred Craddock, *As One Without Authority* (Nashville:Abingdon, 1987), 7.

[4]Morton, *The Journey is Home,* 87.

[5]Carol Lee Flinders, *Enduring Grace: Living Portraits of Seven Women Mystics* (San Francisco: Harper, 1993), 109.

[6]This story was first printed in Mary DonovanTurner, "Word, Words, andWomen," *Setting the Table: Women in Theological Conversation,* ed. Rita Nakashima Brock, Claudia Camp, Serene Jones (St. Louis: Chalice Press, 1995), 219–232.

[7]Smith, *Weaving the Sermon,* 99.

[8]Jean McMahon Humez, *Gifts of Power:The Writings of Rebecca Jackson, Black Visionary, Shaker Eldress* (Amherst: University of Massachusetts Press, 1993), 152–154.

[9]Ibid.

[10]Morton, *The Journey is Home,* 40.

[11]Marjorie Procter-Smith, *In Her Own Rite: Constructing Feminist Liturgical Tradition* (Nashville:Abingdon, 1990), 168.

[12]Morton, *The Journey is Home,* 41.

[13]Hess, "Women's Ways of Preaching," 100.

[14]Dietrich Bonhoeffer, *Schöpfung und Fall* (München: KaiserVerlag, 1955), 57.

[15]Patricia Hill Collins, "The Power of Self-Definition," in *Black Feminist Thought: Knowledge, Consciousness, and the Politics of Empowerment, Perspectives on Gender,* Vol. 2 (New York, London: Routledge, 1991), 92–93,112.

[16]See James H. Evans, Jr., "I Rose and Found MyVoice: Black Church Studies and the Educator," *Theological Education* 21:2 (Spring, 1985): 49–72.

[17]John McClure, "Conversation and Proclamation: Resources and Issues" in *Homiletic* 22:1 (Summer, 1997).

[18]For a further explanation of the exercise, see Joseph D. Driskill, *Protestant Spiritual Exercises:Theology, History and Practice* (Morehouse, 1999), chap. 5.

[19]Christine Smith, "Preaching as an Art of Resistance," in *The Arts of Ministry: Feminist Womanist Approaches,* ed. Christie Cozad Neuger (Louisville:Westminster John Knox, 1996), 41.

[20]Troeger, *The Parable of Ten Preachers,* 39.

[21]Rebecca Chopp, as quoted in Heather Murray Elkins, *Worshiping Women*, 89.

[22]Christine Smith, "Preaching as an Art of Resistance," 48.

[23]William Sloane Coffin, *A Passion for the Possible: A Message to U. S. Churches* (Louisville: Westminster/John Knox Press, 1993), 88.

Chapter 8. Imagining, Listening, Naming: Three Sermons

[1]This text is displayed in the National Civil Rights Museum in Memphis, Tenn.

[2] This sermon was first published in *Pulpit Digest,* March/April 1997, 55–58. Used with permission.

[3]Abraham Maslow, *The Farther Reaches of Human Nature* (New York: Viking Press, 1971), 35–39.

[4]His analysis of the Jonah Complex in the chapter "Flight to Tarshish" shaped my own. See Gregg Levoy, *Callings: Finding and Following an Authentic Life* (Harmony Books, 1997), 206.

Coda

[1]David G. Buttrick, *Homiletic: Moves and Structures* (Philadelphia: Fortress Press, 1987), 452–453.

[2]As quoted in Morton, *The Journey is Home*, 30.

Subject Index

Author Index